JO KIMMEL:

"Many of us are so geared to instant potatoes, instant cement, instant service, and instant this, that, and the other, that we think we can have instant union with God.

"We're very much like one of my daughters who wants to be a singer but who won't go through the disciplines which will give her control of her voice. . . .

"If you want to come into a life of power and peace, joy and creativity, and a life of union where all that's in the Vine can flow through you, there are certain disciplines which must be accepted and practiced.

"Everything I did in the way of discipline was like putting money into a bank. As I needed to draw strength or inner peace or power or whatever, it was there for me to draw from. And there came a day when I badly needed to draw from it, and there it was, treasure I'd stored years and months and days before, ready to pour into me to meet my need.

". . . I now know a state of being in which all tragedy, all suffering, all impatience, all anger — before they become those things — are turned into triumphant, creative living."

STEPS TO PRAYER POWER

JO KIMMEL

ABINGDON  NASHVILLE

STEPS TO PRAYER POWER

A FESTIVAL BOOK

Copyright © 1972 by Abingdon Press
All rights reserved

Festival edition published October 1976.
Second Printing 1980

ISBN 0-687-39340-X

Printed in the United States of America

For Fran, Kay, and Susan
with love

CONTENTS

PREFACE

"Your little increase-decrease prayer has changed my life!" a woman joyfully reported to me recently.

"Your turning-over prayer has really helped me this year," a college student confessed.

"My prayer tree bore fruit in four months."

"My prayer eggs hatched one after another."

"I can now think of the terribly traumatic experiences without hurt because of the healing-of-the-memories prayer."

"Your soaking prayer really works. I soaked my whole family and the love and harmony in our house is almost too good to be true!"

"Jesus has become so real to me through your visualization prayer method, I never feel alone."

With joy I receive such comments as those above in letters and in person. The prayer labs and workshops I've led throughout the country have reached several thousand people. Taped sessions of the labs and workshops have been played and replayed by groups. Men, women, young people, and children are learning new ways in which to pray effectively by experimenting with me in relaxation, visualization, listening, and many other exciting ways to open wide to the love and power of God. It's always marvelous to hear from those who've been to a workshop or lab and discover what they've been doing to block God's power from flowing through them. The sometimes rapid and miraculous changes that take place when the blocks are removed are awe-inspiring, and I never quite get used to what God can do when we allow him to work his will in, to and through us.

Many people have asked me if I've put ideas about prayer into a book. They've said that they wanted to get copies for themselves and their prayer or study groups or simply wanted to hand out copies to friends. Until now I've felt that what I teach depends so much on personal contact in a prayer lab or workshop, that I've wanted to spend my time traveling and holding these. However, I realize that many of you who will read this book might never be able to attend a workshop or lab and because I want to share what I've learned with as wide an audience as I can, I've taken time to gather my thoughts together in book form. The songs that I use in the labs won't get into this book. The really deep personal actions and reactions present during a lab won't be available, but I'm convinced that what I do share will be of help to you, whatever your situation and problem might be.

I've by no means been the originator of all that I use. I've learned from many other people. It would be impossible to name them all, but I would like to acknowledge some such as Glenn Clark, Frank Laubach, Stanley Jones, Agnes Sanford, John Sandford, Tommy Tyson, Marsha and Roland Brown, Tick and Margaret Watson, Gladys McCulloch, Paul Wilkinson, Canon Pearce-Higgins, Louise Eggleston, Bettijune Spiece, Genevieve Parkhurst, Wini Garver, and Pat Helman. A number of ideas have come to me, I feel, through the direct inspiration of the Holy Spirit. Whatever the source they work, and, being a pragmatist I use them and teach them.

In your hands now is a book that can change your life, if you'll experiment with me. Together we'll have our own prayer workshop. It's going to be an exciting adventure—so come pray with me.

RELAXATION
AND PRAYER

Relaxation, physical and mental, is the first step in praying effectively. God is really just waiting to pour into and through us the treasures of heaven, but when we're tense, he can't get through to us. Have you ever had a garden hose which would get a kink in it, and even though you'd turned the faucet on full force, the water couldn't get through that kink? Well, that's often what happens to us; we've a kink, something which has made us tense and worried, and even though we anticipate God's coming to us and blessing us and flowing through us, he can't because of that kink. So the very first thing we need to do in a time of prayer is to relax. Just as we have to walk over and work the kink out of a garden hose, so we must deliberately work the kink out of ourselves before he can flow into and through us. We have to slow down physically and mentally, and this isn't easy. It takes time.

For too long we've thought that prayer is asking God for something. We've planned our day, made out a list, either mentally or on paper, and we've sat down on the edge of a chair and held up our list for God to put his heavenly stamp on, and then off we've gone. But that isn't prayer.

Prayer is making ourselves available to God for his resources and will to flow into and through us. We

11

don't really pray until we're open to him. Sometimes this takes only a minute. Something comes up, and we know instantly that we're incapable of handling it, so we say, "Help, Father," and in that cry, we're open to his resources. Other times, we've worried and wrestled with a problem for weeks; we know there must be a solution, but we haven't been able to work it out. And as each thing we thought of that might work proved ineffective, we've become more worried and desperate until God couldn't possibly get through to help us. We've worked ourselves into a kink. Really there's only one thing to do; begin to work the kink out.

I realize, because I'm a mother with responsibilities and pressures, that most of us are uptight much of the time. We've schedules and deadlines to meet. We're on the run most of the time. When we do have leisure, we don't quite know what to do with it. We vacation to get away from pressures but find new pressures on vacation and often return home more fatigued than when we left. We decide next time to stay at home, and we do—but the children quarrel; the deep freeze suddenly stops working, and we wrap everything in newspaper, hoping we can repair the freezer before everything melts; or we go restlessly from one thing to another, finding no deep satisfaction in the time we have off. We almost long to be back to the everyday routine, for we're more used to coping with the pressures there.

We need to learn to relax. We need to learn how to let go of tension and anxiety and frustration and anything else which keeps us uptight or in a kink.

It's essential to relax, to disconnect with the visible world and its problems, in order to come into an awareness of God and to commune with him. Relaxing the body acts very much as a cleaning agent does on a clogged drain, it loosens and removes whatever blocks the flow of God into and through us. The more relaxed and receptive we become, the easier it is to talk with and to listen to God. The exercises in relaxation in this book are to prepare you to pray more deeply, more effectively, and to enable you to become a wider, deeper channel for God to pour himself through to bless you and others.

Right now check yourself. Are your jaw muscles tight? Is your mind really on this book, or is it darting here and there among your problems? Is your breathing shallow and quick, or is it slow and deep and regular? Is your body in a strained position?

By spending time each day in breathing slowly and deeply and letting go of tensions, we can eventually come to the time when we'll be able to stay in a state of relaxation and calmness all the time.

In the midst of crises or confusion, hurt, or fear, we can act and react from that quiet, relaxed center within which God dwells.

After the first prayer lab I led, I went to stay overnight with a friend. She expected me to be exhausted from a rigorous three-day schedule; however, I was relaxed and refreshed because during the lab we'd relaxed our bodies from tension and released our minds from anxiety. The friend was so impressed, she asked me to let her know when the next lab was to be held, for as a busy mother of four active children, she wanted what I demonstrated. She's attended two labs, and she's applying what she learned to her everyday life and is amazed at how well the techniques work.

One of the techniques which she learned is one I'd like you to experiment with now, if you will. Sit in a comfortable position. Rest your feet on the floor, so there's no strain on either leg. Keep your back straight with shoulders down and back. Lay your hands, palms up, on your thighs. Take in a long, deep breath, and as you exhale, let your head come forward slowly until your chin rests near your chest. Inhale slowly and lift your head, letting it go straight back as far as it will go comfortably, then exhale, letting your head come down slowly to your chest. Do this again making your breathing in and out and the movement of your head slow and regular. Then rest with your head down in front of you and breathe deeply three times, slowly and rhythmically. Now let your head roll over your right shoulder and to the back as you inhale slowly and let it roll on around to your left shoulder and down in front as you exhale slowly. Then reverse the roll. Don't hurry. Take plenty of time and do the roll and reverse roll three times. Feel your jaws relaxing. Feel a yawn in the back of your throat as you do the roll and reverse roll. Keep your shoulders down and relaxed. Only your head should move. Give yourself over to the feeling of quietness that will be coming to you as you breathe and move slowly, regularly, easily. Then lift your head to a comfortable position and with your eyes closed, draw in your breath visualizing that the breath you take in is the peace of God. If you wish, you may say, in your mind, "I draw into my body the peace of God. The peace of God fills me." Then as you exhale slowly, slowly, visualize the peace of God spreading throughout your body. Inhale and exhale three times. Give yourself over to the peace that will be entering into you, and rest. Rest in the awareness of the peace of God in you, breathing slowly and quietly. Just rest.

Experiment with the technique. Reread it until you know what to do and then do it without the strain of trying to keep one eye on the book. Or have a friend read it to you. If you can tape record the experiment, reading slowly and quietly what I've written, then you can play the tape and be free to listen to the instructions. Use the experiment with your prayer partner or your prayer group. You'll find that a wonderful sense of relaxation will come with a little practice.

Most of us don't know what it feels like to be relaxed deeply, and once we discover just how marvelous it is, we'll want to slip into it when we begin to feel tension build up inside us. Not that we dash to sit down and do the head roll and the deep breathing, but we start breathing slowly and rhythmically, letting the muscles in our jaws relax, feeling a yawn in the back of our throats, going on about our business or conversation. As we practice relaxation day after day, we'll discover that it's not too long until it's a habit to be relaxed, and that no matter what happens we're relaxed, calm, and peaceful inside.

I first started experimenting with relaxation when I was in college. One summer I spent two hours each morning from five till seven out on the sundeck. I took along my Bible and a devotional book, and after I was comfortably settled in a chair, I'd read awhile then lay the book aside and "pull the plugs." Then I was ready to pray. I call that summer my golden summer because I never seemed to have to rush or to be under pressure, even though I had what some thought a hectic schedule. I took the maximum number of hours for credit at the college during two regular summer sessions and a third short session, worked as a youth director in a church, and as an office girl in an insurance office. I think that the relaxation in the morning helped me to glide through the day. In subsequent years, "pulling the plugs" has proved as effective as then. I think that you'll enjoy this particular experiment. But I want to warn you that to do it takes a sense of humor. Some groups I've used it with have ended with the giggles. However, after the initial humor of the situation passed, they entered into the experiment with dramatic results.

This experiment takes an active imagination, for you need to visualize that your body is like a crystal tumbler that you can see into, and from the outside you'll be looking at yourself. You'll notice that you're filled with a murky liquid which is a mixture of fear, anxiety, anger, resentment, hate, indecision, physical pain, and negative thoughts. You'll also notice that in the tips of your fingers and toes there are plugs. These are what you'll be pulling out so that the murky liquid can drain out of you. Read through the experiment and get in your mind what you'll be doing because you mustn't keep one eye on the book. You must give yourself over to the visualization and relaxation.

Sit with your feet on the floor, your palms up in your lap, and close your eyes. Then in your imagination see yourself as a crystal tumbler filled with a murky liquid. See the plugs. In your imagination only, bend over and with your right hand pull the plug out of the big toe on your right foot. Hold the plug in your hand and pull the plug out of the next toe and then out of the middle toe, the next toe and finally out of the little one. Lay the plugs down on the floor by your foot. Reach over to the big toe of your left foot and pull the plug out of it, then take the plug from the next toe, the middle toe, the next one, and the little one and lay them on the floor by that foot. Straighten up and with your right hand pull the plug out of your left thumb, out of the index finger, the middle finger, the ring finger, and the little finger. Lay them in your lap. With your left hand, pull the plug from your right thumb, then from the index finger, the middle finger, the ring finger, and the little finger. Lay them in your lap. Now see the murky liquid begin to flow out your fingers and toes slowly. See the level of the liquid move from the very top of your head to your forehead, then down to your nose, then your chin, your neck, your shoulders, out your arms through your hands, and out your fingers. Then see the level of it move down from your chest to your waist, to your hips and thighs, and on down to your knees, the calves of your legs, your ankles, through your feet, and out your toes. This is all down slowly, taking time to visualize the liquid level all the way down through your body. Then imagine that the very top of your head is hinged at the back and that the front part at your forehead lifts up. You see two angels over you with a hose which has a cleansing liquid in it. (Remember I warned you that it takes an active imagination and a sense of humor.) The angels direct the stream of the cleansing liquid into the top of your head, and you feel the swirl of the warm liquid throughout your body, and you see it streaming out your fingers and toes, carrying with it every last little bit of murky liquid that you have in you. Then you feel shining and clean inside. The angels tip the hose up and suddenly they're gone. The top of your head comes back down slowly and you feel refreshed. Then you see the plugs lying on the floor, and you bend over and pick up the five by your right foot and begin to put the plugs back in, first in the big toe, then the next toe, the middle toe, the next one, and the little one. You reach over and pick up five plugs from the floor by your left foot and put one of them in the big toe, one in the next toe, the middle toe, the next one, and the little one. You straighten up and pick up five plugs from your lap. You put one in the thumb of your left hand, one in the index finger, one in the middle finger, one in the ring finger, and one in the little finger. Then you pick up the other five plugs and put one in the thumb of your right hand, one in the index finger, the middle finger, the ring finger, and the little finger.

Now you're ready to be filled. You see over you a huge pitcher which is filled with a beautiful golden liquid. It's a mixture of God's love, light, joy, health, and peace. You open the top of your head, the pitcher tips, and the golden liquid begins to pour into you. You feel it as it trickles down your face, neck, shoulders, chest, hips, thighs, calves, feet. Feel it go down into your toes and see it begin to fill your toes, then your feet. Watch the liquid rise through the calves of your legs, your knees, your thighs, your hips, your waist, your chest, your shoulders, through the shoulders it flows down your arms to your fingertips to fill them and then your hands and lower arms, your elbows, your upper arms, and then on up to your neck and chin, nose, eyes, forehead, until you're completely filled with God's love, light, joy, health, and peace. And you rest, just rest.

The pull-the-plugs experiment is one which people

in the prayer labs or workshops always want repeated when I go back to do a second or third lab. However, not everyone likes it immediately. It may seem foolish or a waste of time. One woman asked for me to repeat the experiment at a second prayer lab in her city. She confessed to us that when we'd done it the first time she hadn't really been able to do it, but four days later she found herself so uptight that she sat down and tried the experiment, and it had worked wonders for her. I hope it does for you, too.

The letting-go experiment can bring deep relaxation to you. Read ahead to get the experiment in mind and then put the book down while you do the things I suggest, using your imagination with the breathing, which should be slow and steady.

Sit quietly and begin to imagine that you're letting go all the tension in your mind. Breathe deeply, and as you breathe out feel that the tension is flowing out of your mind with your breath. Then let go behind your eyes. Breathe out and feel the tension go out from your eyes with your breath. Breathe in, letting go the tension from your ears and jaws, and as you breathe out, feel that tension flow out with the breath. Let your jaws drop a little and feel a yawn in the back of your mouth. If this feels particularly good to you, take several long deep breaths while relaxing in the peace of the moment. Breathe in, and then let go of the tension in the muscles of your neck. Breathe out and feel the tension from your neck go out with the breath. Your head may drop forward or back when the tension goes out, and it relaxes in a comfortable position.

Breathe in now and let go of the tension in your shoulders, breathing out and letting the tension flow with the breath. Then do this again with the shoulders, adding the arms and hands this time in the rhythm of the breathing that you do. Take your time and don't move on to another part of the body until each part has been let go of and relaxed.

Let go in your chest. Feel your heart relaxing, getting into rhythm with the powerful, loving heart of God, and feel the tension flow out of your chest. Breathe deeply.

Let go in your hips, feel the organs in the abdomen relax, let go, so that they can perform their various jobs easily and perfectly, and feel the tension flow out with your breath.

Let go in your thighs, your knees, the calves of your legs, your ankles. Breathe out and feel the tension flowing from your legs.

Let go in your feet and toes. Breathe out and feel all tension flowing from your feet. Then just sit quietly, breathing slowly, easily, aware of a feeling of aliveness, receptivity, and well-being permeating every cell of your body.

No doubt you will adapt these experiments until you find just what works best in your own individual life. The important thing is to take enough time to relax before going into prayer. The more you practice the relaxation of your body and mind, the easier it becomes. Master relaxation of body and mind, and you'll be thrilled with the new depth that your prayer life will take on.

There is one more experiment which I want to share with you, which more and more people are using, and it will lead us into the next chapter on visualization. I include it in here because it's primarily used to bring about relaxation.

Picture Jesus standing in front of you. See him kneel beside you and look deeply into your eyes. What love and compassion you see in his eyes. What understanding for you and your problems you see in his eyes. A great longing wells up within you to be as a little child so that Jesus might take you on his lap and comfort you. Then you see that you are a little child and that Jesus picks you up and then sits down, holding you on his lap. You rest your head against his broad shoulder. You feel the rather rough texture of his robe against your cheek. You feel enveloped by understanding love and acceptance. All tension just melts in the warmth of his love. As a child who has been frightened finds peace in his father or mother, so now you find peace in Jesus and you rest in him, secure. Now that you've learned to relax, you're ready to pray.

VISUALIZATION PRAYER

Visualization prayer is probably one of the most exciting kinds of praying we can do. God's given us a wonderful gift in our imagination. We use our imaginations continually. For instance, did you ever find yourself replaying a scene in your mind in which someone said something rude to you, and even though you didn't respond at the time, now in your imagination you say what you think of the person and see yourself getting the better of him? How about a situation which went all wrong, did you play and replay the scene over and over, experiencing the embarrassment again and again? Well, this is a destructive use of the imagination. In visualization prayer, we deliberately use the imagination in a constructive way for ourselves and for others. As we consciously make good pictures in our minds, we train our subconscious minds to work for us in a constructive way until it becomes habitual or natural for us to have our conscious minds filled with thoughts that are true, pure, lovely, gracious, and honorable, just as Paul suggests we do (Philippians 4:8.)

Let me make it clear that in visualization prayer we're not trying to manipulate a reluctant God into doing something for us he doesn't want to do. Rather we're seeking to allow God to work in and through us, changing us and our ideas concerning a person or situation if need be. It's very important to understand

21

this so that we can then pray confidently, expectantly, and with power.

A woman I know needed to get away from her family for awhile. I offered to let her have the money she needed to pay someone to come in and be house-keeper and babysitter and cook and to pay for a week at a cabin in a state park so she could get away from her problems and get a better perspective on them. The understanding was that she would repay me the small sum as soon as she could. She said she'd let me know when she could arrange it. In a week she called, saying that a member of her family was terribly sick and she needed to go to them and had no money, would I be willing to give her money for that trip? I said that I would and asked her how much she needed. When she answered five hundred dollars I was startled but told her that I'd send her a check imme-diately. She assured me that she would repay me as soon as possible, which wouldn't be long. I sent the money at once.

I saw her only occasionally over the next few years, and each time she assured me that she would repay me. I'd think about her and the five hundred dollars which I could have used to advantage many times, and become quite upset that she hadn't paid any-thing back. I'd go over and over the phone conversation, thinking that I should have said, "I can only send you two hundred dollars and I'll have to have it repaid in six months," or, "I'm really sorry but I just can't let you have the money." Finally I realized what my play-ing and replaying the phone conversation was doing to me. I was angry with myself for having been taken in by her, I lost faith in lending anyone money, and most of all I was in inner turmoil because I wasn't being paid back and felt resentful about it. I knew I had to deal with myself somehow. I prayed about the situation, and it seemed that I should write her and tell her that I was surprised that I hadn't heard from her about the money by this time. I told her of some financial needs I would be facing in the future and how what she owed me would take care of them. I really like the woman, and so there was nothing harsh about what I said to her. I mailed the letter and felt a release, but then I sat down and imagined her receiving the letter, reading it, and then trying to figure out how she could begin to repay me. I saw her face light up with joy as she worked out how she would repay me without working a hardship on her own finances. I just thanked God that the debt would be repaid in the right way and at the right time. Whenever I thought of the situation again, I just thanked God that he was working out his will in it—there was no more playing and replaying of what might have been.

Not long after I sent the letter, I had a most cordial note from the woman, and she enclosed a check for fifty dollars. She said she was sorry that she hadn't sent me any money before, and that now that bills were caught up she could send me fifty dollars twice a month until the debt was paid. Needless to say, I rejoiced. However, nothing came from her at the end of two weeks, yet at the end of a month, there was a money order for one hundred dollars. But that was all. I haven't hear from her since then. I'm not stewing about it. I'm seeing her joyfully sending me money until the debt is fully paid. I'm sure that this is what she wants as well as what I want.

Often when we use the imagination destructively, we close off part of our heart to other people, and we feel only great weight when we think of them.

I heard of a woman who quarreled with her son about something he'd done. She couldn't forgive him. She told him to leave home and never come back. He left and sometime later the mother experienced the love of Jesus. She then realized that she needed to forgive her son, but somehow it wasn't in her power to do this. She just didn't have room in her heart for him. Finally, in prayer, she said, "Jesus, I know that you're a carpenter, and I give you permission to build a room in my heart for my son."

Jesus began to do just that—to build a room in her heart for her son—and there came a time when she could forgive her son, and they were reconciled.

If there's someone for whom there's no room in your heart and you know that there should be, sit quietly, relax, and visualize Jesus, strong, capable, a skilled craftsman, standing before you. Confess to him that you don't have room in your heart for that person and give him permission to build a room in your heart for him or her. Then when you think of that person, don't waste emotion in a negative way by feeling a closed heart. Simply remind yourself that Jesus is building a room for him in your heart, and then visualize that this is what Jesus is doing, ever so gently, lovingly, and beautifully. Jesus has the ability to build rooms in our hearts for others. He can also melt our hearts from hardness toward others.

A man I know was, I thought, very unjust in his treatment of a very good friend of mine. I thought the man was completely unchristian in what he did to my friend. Every time I thought of the man I'd see a whitewashed tomb with decay inside it. I didn't like to be around the man, but there were times that I had to be. He was always cordial, sometimes, I felt, too sickeningly cordial, putting on a show for those around him. I continually condemned the man when I thought of him until one day I realized that I'd cut myself off from a fellow human being by my judgmental attitude toward him, and I remembered the words from I John 4:20-21: "If any one says 'I love God,' and hates his brother, he is a liar; for he who does not love his brother whom he has seen, cannot love God whom he has not seen." I knew that my heart needed to be melted so that I could love that man. I also knew that I couldn't do it, so I asked Jesus to melt my heart and let his love and my love flow to the man. I sat quietly, visualizing that my heart was being melted by the love of Jesus and that love was just streaming out of my heart to the man. I didn't try to love the man, I simply let the love flow through me and somehow in the flowing of Jesus' love, my love flowed, too. I can now think of the man without the resentment and contempt I'd felt for so long. And now, I often ask God to let me channel his love and blessing to this man.

If there's someone you resent or hate or feel contempt for, sit quietly, relax, rest, wait, then visualize Jesus standing in front of you, looking at you with compassion and understanding and tell him how you feel about the person. Tell him you know this feeling keeps you from receiving all the good you can from him. Ask him to melt your heart with his love. Then visualize your heart being melted by his love and that love flowing out from you. See the stream of love flowing to the person you've let come between you and God. Just let it flow for awhile and then end your visualization prayer with gratitude for your imagination and for what Jesus has done in melting your heart and letting love flow through you.

It may be there's more than one person you've been separated from, and this would be a good time to see the love flowing to others who have hurt you or misunderstood you and whom you've misunderstood. Take your time with each one. Keep your breathing deep and regular and your body relaxed. Never hurry this process, rather let it flow slowly from you.

I use visualization prayer a great deal in prayer labs or workshops. It's a powerful way in which to pray and sometimes leads someone who doesn't really know Jesus personally into a deep experience with him.

A woman wrote me almost a year after a prayer lab and said that during our visualization of Jesus he'd suddenly really been there, and because he was, she had a deep spiritual experience. From what more she said, that was just the beginning of a new way of living for her which has grown better as the days have gone by.

For this particular visualization of seeing Jesus, grow very quiet inside. Let your breathing be light and easy and regular. Be in a waiting, a listening, attitude. Then picture Jesus in front of you. See how tall he is and what he's wearing. Look at his hands, his feet, and then his face. Look deeply into his eyes, then notice the texture of his skin. Does he have a smile? Is his hair brushed back from his face? Take in all the details that you can, slowly, and rest in his presence. Walk along beside him; feel his hand on your shoulder. Share silence with him, and then walk on until you come to a place where you can sit together and talk. Tell him whatever is troubling you and tell him that you want and welcome his help. Assure him that whatever he feels would work out the best in your situation will be fine with you. And then thank him that he already has begun to work your problem out.

Why not now bring to Jesus someone you know who needs help? Visualize that person walking toward the two of you. See Jesus and yourself rise to greet the person, and you make the introduction by saying, "Jesus this is N——; N——, this is Jesus." Draw aside then, and leave the two of them together. See them talking with each other. See the face of the person you introduced to Jesus light up with joy during the conversation. If the person has something physically wrong with him, see Jesus stretch forth his hand and lay it on the person, and see the person made whole, filled with strength and joy. Take plenty of time to visualize. Watch the person you introduced to Jesus, restored and released into a new life, going on his way, and then bring another person and introduce him to Jesus and see a similar thing happen. Bring as many people as you will to Jesus and let him meet their needs.

In the type of visualization you've been doing just now there is relinquishment, for you don't stay around and try to tell Jesus what to do for the person. You just trust him to know what is best, and you trust that he will do it.

A woman who'd been unable to pray effectively for her son found this method in which she could really release him. His problems began to work out almost immediately. She stood by him, not offering advice, but offering inner gratitude for what Jesus can do when allowed to come into a person's life.

You see, you can actually keep God from working his will in another's life by your worry, your continual advice, which often wasn't asked for in the first place, and by your always seeing the negative traits of the person. Think of that. The great God of the universe, who created it and sustains it, can be blocked by you. Do you see what you've been doing in trying to tell another what is best for him? You've been saying really that he is unacceptable to you as he is and that he should change and change in the way that you say.

I know you love him, that you want what's best for him, but your idea of what's best for him may not be God's idea. Your motives may be good, but your methods aren't. For instance, someone you love very much smokes. You're worried that he'll get lung cancer or throat cancer, and you continually let him know, either verbally or nonverbally, that you want him to quit smoking, that you love him and want him to live, and that you think his life may be shortened if he smokes. Somehow it seems to be human nature to meet resistance with resistance. Perhaps your bringing the conversation around to his smoking only makes him want to prove to you that he is himself, in charge of his life, that even though he loves you, he won't let you pressure him into changing. Well, if the way you've been trying hasn't worked, why keep on with it? Try this experiment: Sit quietly, relax, breathe deeply and slowly, then picture Jesus in front of you. Bring that loved one to Jesus and introduced him to Jesus then leave them alone. After they've been together a little time, see them walk off together, Jesus' hand on the shoulder of the one you brought to him. And then thank and praise Jesus that he's having his way with the loved one. Everyday, then, as often as you need to, just say, "Thank You, Jesus, that you're taking care of N——. Thank You." Never again say anything to the person about his smoking. If you find yourself getting tense inside because you see him light up a cigarette or cigar, say in your mind, "Thank You, Jesus, that you're taking care of him. Thank you," and quietly relax inside by breathing deeply.

In college, I had a professor who was a really wonderful person. I asked him once why he continued to smoke when he knew it wasn't good for him, for I'd heard him say he felt it wasn't. He answered that it was a habit, and anyway, he liked it. I didn't say anything more to him about it, but I did the visualization which I've shared with you, and each time I thought of him, I thanked Jesus for taking care of him. Summer school ended and I went home for a few days. When I returned to enroll that fall, the professor was the first person I saw on campus. He came toward me smiling and saying accusingly, "You've been praying for me."

"Why," I said innocently, "What in the world do you mean?"

"I've stopped smoking!" he said triumphantly.

Now you may not always get the neat little wrap-up to the story such as I got in that particular situation. For instance, you may just get to the place where you no longer see that smoking or not smoking is all that important.

Each person is answerable for himself ultimately. This doesn't mean that we just sit with hands folded. We try to help others, but if they don't want our help, we should be willing to leave them alone. The attitude of "I'm going to help you if it kills you" just isn't the attitude for the Christian. We can trust Jesus enough to place a person in his hands and we thank him that his will's being done in, to, and through this person.

And even in the face of what seems to be the exact opposite of what we might want for the person, we still say, "Thank you. I know that you're taking care of him."

There's now another visualization experiment I'd like to share with you. This experiment I call the pool prayer.

First, of course, relax, breathe deeply and regularly, and grow quiet inside. Take your time to do this. Then imagine a ray of light shining down on you. It's a ray of white light and feels warm and comfortable to you as it shines on you. Rest in the relaxing warmth of it and feel it penetrating into every cell of your body, until you're aglow with the light. Picture it radiating from you, forming a pool of light in front of you. It is deep and clear. When the image is strong—and take time to see it and enjoy it—bring someone you want to pray for to the pool. See him walk into it or jump into or dive into it. Somehow, as you do this particular experiment, the persons you bring to the pool take on a life of their own as they walk with you to the pool, and you'll often find that they'll enter the pool in unexpected ways. Let them, and watch as they eventually become submerged in the pool of light. Then you're ready to bring another and watch him or her, then another and another, never hurrying the images or leaving out some of the steps, but taking time to see the action of the scene unfold before your inner eyes.

When you've brought all the persons to the pool that you want to bring, then bring your church, the minister and congregation, bring your city, your state, your nation, and the world. End your experiment with words such as these: "Thanks so much, Father, that I could bring these people and situations to you. Thank you that your healing light is meeting the needs in each one. Thanks."

As you experiment with visualization prayer, there will come ideas for visualization which are seemingly inspired. I lead several groups a week in prayer and meditation, and I really never have anything prepared for us to do. I always feel that as we open to God, his creativity will flow into us, and all the ideas we need will be given to us. Not long ago a group was meeting in my home, and after we'd sung some choruses about Jesus, we all grew very still. I closed my eyes and with my inner eyes, I saw Jesus standing in front of me. Somehow his great love reached out to me, and I felt all negative emotions being drawn out from me. As this happened, I thought of a powerful magnet which draws filings to it. I felt fatigue and problems being drawn out of me, and then I felt completely empty, but only for a few seconds, because then I began to feel power, strength, peace, love, and joy emanating from Jesus. These flowed into me until I felt filled with energy and happiness.

It suddenly occurred to me that what I'd experienced could be experienced by each person in the prayer group, and so quietly I shared with the others what I'd experienced and suggested we visualize Jesus doing the same thing to each person in the group. We took time to do this, then we visualized his doing the same for people we knew, for our churches, our city, our state, and our world. It took about an hour for us to do this. We were all refreshed and renewed at the end of the hour.

You can use this particular experiment in visualization prayer when you're weary or sad or depressed or in pain. Sit quietly and visualize Jesus with you drawing the weariness, the sadness, the depression, the pain from you; emptying you. Then see the peace, the power, the wholeness, the strength, the love, or the joy flowing from him to you and rest in it as it fills you completely.

Jesus said that he's with us always. Most of us aren't yet well enough attuned to see him or sense him with us. Visualization prayer helps us open our inner eyes to the reality of the presence of Jesus.

RELINQUISHMENT PRAYER

There are a number of prayers that can be grouped
together under the title of relinquishment prayers for
that in essence is the idea underlying them all.

I'll be sharing with you a number of personal experiences, because I have used this particular type of
prayer more than any other kind. In fact, I've used it
so much that it has become an almost automatic response when something comes up.

I was informed by my daughter, Kay, one day that,
following a long weekend, her class at school would
have to start meeting on a split-session for the rest of
the year. Tuesday she'd be in the afternoon section.
My heart sank. I write in the morning after the girls
go to school. Susan, my youngest daughter, had been
on a split-session all year and she arrived home at one.
Kay, on an afternoon schedule, would leave home
about noon and not return until about six.

I called the school at once and asked for the principal only to discover that he was in a meeting and
was leaving immediately after for the weekend. The
office girl said she'd have him call me as soon as he
could. There was no call by Tuesday morning, and I
decided to drive to school and talk with him. On the
way to school I began to pray about the situation. I'd
been so sure that Kay should be in the morning session
that I hadn't even bothered to pray about the situation.

31

But as I drove, I thought, "Father, do you have some reason why Kay's been put in the afternoon session? Does she need to be with me more and is this the best way to arrange it? Maybe you did work it out so that she and I could spend more time together. Well, I just want to thank you that what's best for Kay will work out. I don't have to write. She's far more important to me than any article or book," and as I talked to God, a feeling of peace settled inside me. Somehow I knew that whatever did work out would be for the best, and I became happy thinking that Kay might be staying home mornings.

I had to wait in the office because another woman was in talking to the principal. I sat quietly, just thanking God that his will was being done. Then I was called into the inner office. The principal knew me because I'd helped with a number of bake sales at the school and he greeted me cordially. I told him that I wanted to talk with him about Kay and her being assigned to an afternoon session.

"I'm a widow and a writer. My only time to write is in the morning. I already have a daughter in the morning session, and I was wondering if Kay might be transferred to the morning session, too?"

"Well," he said, "I don't see any reason why we can't put her in a morning class. Would you like a man teacher for her?"

This was more than I had expected. The girls weren't around men very much. Most of my friends were women, either single, widowed, or those who were married and had time during the day to shop or lunch or go to prayer groups. I said, delightedly, "That would be just wonderful. The girls aren't around men very much."

"Well, now, would you like a little man or a big man?" he asked smiling.

"Tell me about them," I said, thinking, "Father, you're really too much! Here Kay will be in a morning session with a man teacher, and I even get to choose the size of the teacher. You're just full of surprises, and I do thank you."

The principal told me about the men, and they both seemed fine to me, but I said, "Let's try the big man's class."

"Good," he said. "See that she gets to school this morning and have her take this to her teacher," and he handed me a note which he'd filled in while talking. I shook his hand and thanked him and then sang all the way home.

I'd relinquished my desire to have the mornings in which to write, and I'd been ready to accept anything. He'd given much more than I'd have dreamed of asking. He's that way. The measure of goodness he gives is filled up, pressed down, running over. I'm often willing to settle for less than he wants to give. I've discovered that even the most wonderful things I can think of seem pale and lifeless beside what he wants for me.

About the time the Doctor Dolittle movie was popular, my daughter Susan had a birthday. For weeks before the party she kept pestering me about making a three-tiered birthday cake. It seemed every time I turned around there she was, asking me about the three-tiered cake. Finally, I looked into her eyes and said, "You know, Susan, I heard you the very first time that you asked for the special birthday cake. I've told you repeatedly that you'll have it. Now if you say another word to me about it, I won't make it for you at all."

She didn't mention the cake to me again, but from time to time I heard her tell Fran and Kay that she was going to have a three-tiered cake for her birthday.

The day of her birthday, I made a three-tiered cake, iced it with green frosting and put little plastic figures of Doctor Dolittle and the animals all over it. It was just delightful. I blew up several dozen balloons and hung them in clusters above the dining room table and the archway leading into the dining room, and strung red, rose, and pink crepe paper streamers from each corner of the room to the center light-drop and over to the archway balloons. When Susan came in after school and saw the decorations her face shone with happiness. The cake and decorations were far more exciting than any she'd dreamed of.

What I did for Susan, God does for us. He takes our desires the first time we express them, and then he begins to work to bring about what we've desired. However, if we continually ask him again and again for what we've already ased, he's not free to continue to work but must listen and listen to us, and we're asking and asking when we should be joyously going about our business, glad that our desire is being fulfilled in the right way and at the right time.

It is often we ourselves who keep us from our own good because we want to see results right away, and we want the results to be what we think is best.

I'm learning to be open always to something better than what I feel I want and to say, "If you have something better for me, I'll take that!"

I believe that God wants us to ask for things, but I also believe that we need to keep open-ended toward whatever else God's prepared for us.

Sometimes God does just the reverse of what we think we need. For instance, one time I went to the hospital to call on a woman in our church. Ted, my husband, was with her awhile, and I stayed with our daughters in the car. When he came out, I went in and talked with her. She was sitting up in bed gasping for breath. "Pray for," she gasped, "my release." I knew immediately that she was asking for me to pray that she'd die. I took her hand and said, "I can't. But I will pray God's will be done in you." I did and then asked if she'd like me to say the Twenty-third Psalm. She wanted me to and even tried to say part of it with me. I leaned over and kissed her and left.

I was in the city two days later, and as I was going into a store, the woman was coming out. I almost fell over when I saw her. She said the doctor had discovered and corrected a pinched nerve in her neck, and she'd been released from the hospital that day.

Sometimes we think we're praying right and discover that we're not at all. A friend and I had been using a visualization prayer for her mother, who was in a nursing home being treated for pneumonia. We'd visualize strength and health pouring into her, see her get out of bed, dress, ride home, and settle into her little apartment. Then one day, with my eyes closed but my inner eyes open, I saw the mother. She came hesitantly toward me and I heard her say, "Won't you please release me?" then she disappeared. I shared with my friend what I had seen, and we agreed that we'd no longer use the visualization prayer but that we'd simply put the mother in God's hands, relinquish her, and ask that this will be done whatever it was. The friend called me the next morning to tell me that her eighty-year-old mother has passed very easily from life to Life during the night.

It's often very difficult to come to the place where we can relinquish someone or something. We feel we know what's best. We've not yet learned that God is a loving father who desires only good for us, his children. If we do make the act of relinquishment, we often take back what we relinquish and become concerned about it again. In this prayer there must be no taking back what we relinquish. Each time a thought of the object comes into the mind, we must remind ourselves that we've relinquished that into God's hands and he's taking care of it, even if we have to do it a hundred times a day.

It's good to add visualization to relinquishment. I like to picture Jesus standing in front of me, looking at me with compassion, waiting for me to respond to him. I take my problem, as though I have it in my hands, and I tell him everything I can think about it. I then see myself handing it over to him, simply turning it over to him to take care of in the best way at the best time. Then I remind myself when I think of it that I turned it over to him and he's working on it.

A friend came to see me one day. She was intensely troubled. After sharing deeply with me, she and I turned the problem over to Jesus by visualizing her handing the problem over to him. Suddenly my visualization took on life of its own, and I saw Jesus put the problem down, pick up an axe, and chop it into little pieces as though to say, "It won't bother you anymore. I've taken care of it." This proved to be true.

Visual aids can be helpful in relinquishment. I've used the "prayer tree" and the "prayer eggs" for many years and find that somehow my subconscious knows I mean business when I use them. It's easy to believe that the tree will bear fruit in its own season and that the eggs will hatch in the required number of days.

The prayer tree comes from Glenn Clark in his book, *I Will Lift up Mine Eyes.* It's made by taking a sheet of paper and drawing the base of the tree, the trunk and then three branches. Write "love" at the base, "the kingdom of God" on the trunk, and then "people" on one branch, "places" on a second, and "things" on the third. Make lines out from the branches and write the people you'd like to know and be associated with, either individual names or the types of persons you want to become friends with. For instance, when we lived in the country in a parsonage and I had contact with few people, I drew a prayer tree, and one of the desires I put on the people-branch was "people I can share my faith with and who'll share theirs with me." Within a week, I was phoned by the local home economics teacher who asked me if I would talk to the local Future Homemakers of America group on the topic, "Foundations Today Make Homes of Tomorrow." I accepted with alacrity and was able to tell the girls of the importance of having a strong spiritual foundation to help them as homemakers. They liked what I said and recommended that I speak to the district FHA meeting. I did and received many invitations from FHA chapters throughout our area.

Churches and civic organizations heard from them that I was avilable as a speaker and my contacts widened. I addressed the state convention of the Future Home-makers in Illinois and spoke on the topic, "Guided Misses." As a result of that talk, I received invitations throughout the state to speak. My people-branch certainly bore fruit and in a hurry.

On the places-branch put the various places that you'd really like to visit or live. There've been times when I've crossed off certain places that I wrote on the branch, because as time passed, the desire to go there simply vanished. But one time I had written on the places-branch, "England, France, and India." Circumstances worked out that I could spend six weeks abroad, and I was in England a week, France a week, and in India four weeks. Those six weeks were very rewarding because I was studying prayer and healing, and I feel that I learned a great deal.

On the things-branch, put both material and spiritual things. For instance, you need and want a new coat; surely you can put that on. But how about being clothed with patience? Don't you really need that, too? Well, you can write that down on the things-branch. You need a new car to get around in? Put that down, and then see if you need to have your feet shod with the sandals of peace. Put peace down, too. I've discovered that usually everything we want in the material world has a counterpart in the spiritual world. Check to see what your material needs and wants are and then look to see what their spiritual counterparts are. Write down both.

After you've made the prayer tree put it in your Bible at the First Psalm where it says, "He is like a tree planted by streams of water, that yields its fruit in its season." You've planted your tree now, and you can be sure that God will bring forth the right fruit at the right season. Whenever something you have put on your tree comes to mind, just think, "God is bringing forth in its own season," and leave it at that.

The prayer eggs are similar to the prayer tree and again the idea comes from Glenn Clark. You take a sheet of paper and draw some ovals or eggs on it, and inside each oval write a desire. Cut the eggs out and put them in the Bible at Matthew 23:37 where it says, "How often would I have gathered your children together as a hen gathers her brood under her wings, and you would not," and let them hatch. As you think about the eggs you've set to hatch, you may want to take some out and throw them away or add a few others. Remind yourself when you think of any of your desires that they'll hatch at the right time.

A very simple but very meaningful relinquishment prayer is what I call the soaking prayer. Tick Watson shared this type prayer with a group of us one night. It is one of the most delightful ways that I've found. You simply picture a pool of God's love and blessing, and you bring people into it, watch them become submerged, and leave them soaking. This is best done at night as you are ready to sleep. All the people you bring bring into the pool soak all night long. I also like to immerse my whole house and everyone in it in the pool before I fall asleep. I feel safe and happy knowing that we're soaking in God's love and blessing all night.

The increase-decrease prayer is another type of relinquishment prayer. I learned about it a long time ago. I was talking with a woman at a Camp Farthest Out and telling her that I didn't know just what I would do after I finished college. She said, "Why don't you try the increase-decrease prayer?"

"What's the increase-decrease prayer?" I asked because I'd never heard of it.

"It works like this," she said. "You have something you think you'd like to do, but you don't know for sure if it's God will for you to do it, so you simply say, 'Father, if I'm to do this, increase the desire within me to do it and if I'm not to do it, decrease the desire within me,' and that's all there is to it. You'll know—

oh maybe not just that minute, but within a few days or weeks—whether the desire is increased or decreased, and you take that as your guidance."

It certainly sounded simple enough and I tried it. It was simple but the results were astonishing. It really worked time after time as I used it. After college I went to British Columbia to help at a Canadian Guild of Health Camp and also at a Camp Farthest Out and then went on down into California to a CFO. Subsequently, I was led to enter Brethren Volunteer Service where I met Ted Kimmel, married him four months after we met, honeymooned in Europe and the Middle East, and settled in Baghdad, Iraq.

There are variations on the increase-decrease prayer. You'll find your own according to your situation just as I did.

We had a country pastorate during Ted's last year of seminary. He was in school all week and came out to the parsonage and church on weekends. He'd become very interested in photography, and he was in a position, financially, to buy equipment. He had an excellent camera, and he outfitted a darkroom in the basement of the parsonage. When he was home on weekends, he spent his time making calls on church families and in taking and developing and printing pictures. He spent no time with the family except at meals, and often he was late for them. I became, to put it mildly, indignant that he was spending so much time with other people and photography, and I prayed that either he would get sick and tired of photography and sell everything he had or that I'd learn to like photography. I must admit that I was certain he'd grow sick and tired of photography, but, you know, as the days went by, gradually I became so interested in picture taking, developing, and printing that I'd take our three daughters and go down into the darkroom with Ted and help him. It became absolutely fascinating to adjust the enlarger, push the button, lift off the sheet of paper and put it in the developer, and watch the faces or trees or whatever begin to emerge.

My variation of the increase-decrease prayer had worked, but not as I'd anticipated it would. I never again felt even the least resentment toward Ted about his photography, and when we moved to New York City and he registered his work as Christian Photographers, I often helped him supply prints to magazines. It really became a source of deep satisfaction to work alongside him, and of course, the extra income wasn't hard to take.

The increase-decrease prayer or variations of it have worked time after time in my life and in the lives of many people who have been to the prayer labs where I teach it. Its simplicity throws some people, particularly those whose lives are very complex. They can't believe that so simple a prayer could work. They've been pleasantly surprised when they've tried it and found it works.

When we lived in New York City, Ted was offered three different jobs in the Africa area. He had an interesting and challenging job as a youth editor with Friendship Press of the National Council of Churches, and I was in a doctoral program in Speech and Drama at Teachers College, Columbia University. We really didn't want to go abroad, but when the third offer came, we looked at each other and thought, "Is God trying to tell us that he wants us in the Africa area?" So we prayed the increase-decrease prayer. Within three days, we knew, each independently of the other, that the desire had been increased. Then we prayed that the desire would be increased to accept the job God wanted us to have and that the desire for the other two would decrease. Again, within three days each of us knew we were to accept Church World Service offer to work on the island of Madagascar. Ted resigned from his position, I dropped some classes and finished my master's degree, and we set out for Madagascar.

If you have a decision to make and don't know just

what to do, try the increase-decrease prayer. If you really want to know what to do and are willing to have your desire either increased or decreased, it'll work for you. In the years I've used it and taught others to use it, I and others have only praise for the simple little prayer. I pray that you'll find it as exciting as I have.

SUBCONSCIOUS PRAYER

In a way, the title of the chapter is deceptive because what I'll be talking about isn't really prayer in a strictly defined sense of talking with God but in a broader sense of making yourself available to God to use in the life of another person.

It was from Louise Eggleston that I first heard about subconscious prayer. She told just how she used it. I sat spellbound for an hour eagerly hoping that she'd just keep on talking, the story she told was so fascinating.

I've had the opportunity to use it several times in working with people who didn't respond to any other type of prayer. It is a type of prayer that should be used with discretion, generally only when all else has failed to bring a response. I'll point out one of the dangers concerning the use of it later. But first let me tell you of a personal experience I had in using subconscious prayer.

My husband had died and my daughters and I had moved to Indiana where I was to teach in a church-related college. My youngest daughter who was seven years old had started taking money which belonged to her sisters. She'd also take money from my purse. I simply couldn't make her understand that it wasn't hers to take and use. I prayed about it in all the ways that I could think of, and nothing seemed to work.

Also, she'd gotten to the place where she hated to get up in the morning. It was difficult to get her into decent clothes and get her off to school in the morning. Then she began simply taking over the conversation whenever people came to talk with me. She was terribly obnoxious, and I thought of asking my mother if she could take Susan to live with her for a while. When I confided in a friend, she suggested that I take her to a psychiatrist, but somehow there was that within me that knew Susan would respond if only I could find the right way to pray for her. Then I remembered Louise Eggleston's subconscious prayer and decided to try it.

That night after I was in bed I plumped the pillow up, took pencil and paper and asked God to give me the right words to say to Susan's subconscious mind. I was still for a long time. Then the first thought which came to mind was, "Mommy loves you." Did I ever have to wrestle with that one. I knew that deep down I must love her, but somehow I'd buried the love under a lot of criticism, anger, frustration, hopelessness, and impatience. Finally, and it took quite a while, I became willing to uncover it and use that love. So with a feeling that I'd throw away those negative attitudes I'd held about Susan, I wrote on the paper, "Mommy loves you." Then the next thoughts flowed and I wrote them down, "Fran loves you; Kay loves you; God loves you; Jesus loves you. You're going to be loving and gentle and kind and patient like Jesus." That was all. That didn't seem like much, but I knew that if I used that for at least a month, something had to happen for good in Susan.

I set the alarm clock for three o'clock and went to sleep. Now there's no magic in three o'clock, but I knew she'd be fast asleep then. When the alarm rang, I turned it off, switched on the light, and sleepily tried to read what I'd written earlier. When my eyes focused enough, I called quietly, but aloud three times, "Susan Elaine Kimmel." This was to attract the subconscious mind of Susan. Now, she was in her room and I was in mine with the door shut. Then I repeated what I'd written three times, set the alarm for six when I had to get up, switched off the light, and fell asleep. At six I got up, dressed, slipped over to the college chapel lounge, and met with a group of students who came to pray together five mornings a week. When I returned home a little after seven, Susan met me at the door. She was dressed for school and welcomed me with a cheery, "Breakfast is ready!" and led me into the dining room. Sure enough, there was the table beautifully set and I saw sausage, scrambled eggs with parsley sprinkled on them, orange juice, toast, jam, and tea. Need I say that I was stunned? I couldn't believe my eyes. What was before me was too good to be true. I looked into Susan's little upturned, shining face then enveloped her in a big hug. "Oh, Susan, this is wonderful. Everything looks marvelous."

The subconscious prayer had worked and had worked overnight. It had far exceeded my expectations. But, just to make sure that the thing was clinched, I set the alarm for three o'clock for the next twenty-nine days and read the message to Susan's subconscious. Some five years later, I could say that only once did she slip back into the old habits, but I got the message out and for three nights read it to her, and she's been fine since then.

A woman heard me tell this story at a prayer lab, and she immediately identified her son with Susan. She began to use the subconscious prayer. I returned to her city a year later and was asked by her to relate the story to the group at the prayer lab. I did, and then the woman told how she'd been using this type prayer for months and hadn't seen any results until about three months before our meeting. Since then, there'd been steady progress in her son. She said that she'd use the prayer until she felt her son was completely free from the anxieties and problems he had. We could but rejoice with her that at long last her son was responding.

There is a danger, of course, in talking to the sub-conscious of someone, as no doubt, you've already perceived. It's this: We don't always know what is best for another person, and we need to be extremely careful in what we say to the subconscious. We need to be in a prayerful attitude and ask God to bring into our minds what would be best to say to the person. We may want to manipulate others to make situations convenient for ourselves and so we must guard against this kind of thing happening. After all, it may be *we* who need changing. So always ask for more light into your own motives and ask God to align them with his will.

We can deceive ourselves into thinking that a situation would be better if another person would change. We tend to think that we don't need to change. However, as you begin to keep yourself in a state of openness Godward, he will begin to reveal to you just what and how you yourself, need to change, and then he'll give you the power to do so.

If you want to use the subconscious prayer, look into yourself first and be prepared for the kind of purging such as I experienced when I knew I hadn't been feeling or showing love to Susan and had to battle that one out.

Ask God to reveal to you your own responsibility in the situation or with the person and wait. Then take whatever thoughts come to you and say, "Thank you, Father. Please expand them," and wait. You'll be shown what you need to do or not do. Ask that if you're to help the other person by using the sub-conscious prayer that the desire within you will be increased to do so, and if you're not to, that the desire will be decreased. Perhaps you'll know just then if you're to use it or not. Perhaps you won't know for a few days, but keep reminding yourself that God is increasing or decreasing the desire according to his will. When you get the answer and if it's that you aren't to help the other person by using the subconscious prayer, just say, "Thanks for showing me your will." But if the desire has increased within you, take pencil and paper and ask God to bring thoughts to your mind for you to write down and then wait.

As the thoughts come, write them down and then check them against what you know of the love and understanding of Jesus. Is there any sentence that sounds as though it couldn't have been spoken by Jesus? If so, ask God to clarify what he means. You will eventually receive just the right words to speak into the subconscious of the person. Then when you know that the person's asleep and can't hear your voice, call his full name three times and read aloud three times what you've written. Do this only once a day. During the day when you think about the person remember not to worry but to say, "Thanks, Father, for him." Use the prayer only until you feel led to stop it. The woman in the prayer lab had used it for some nine months before she began to see any results.

Results sometimes come quickly and sometimes come slowly. One woman used it on her husband, who was an alcoholic and discovered that it was upsetting him and causing him to drink more. But when she talked with me, she discovered why. In her zeal to help him, she had typed six copies of what she was reading into his subconscious and had given them to praying friends, who were as zealous as she and who took turns during the night to read the message aloud. The poor man was being bombarded all night long with suggestions. He awakened every morning more exhausted than when he went to bed. I pointed this out to the woman and recommended that she alone speak to his subconscious and only once a day. When she did this he began to become more relaxed without having to use alcohol. The woman also began to see what she could do to change herself into a less judgmental and a more loving person. I haven't heard from the woman in several years, and I assume that her problem has worked out satisfactorily. Somehow I'm the first to hear if it hasn't and the last to hear if it has.

I have one last suggestion concerning the subconscious prayer. It can be tied in very well with the healing-of-the-memories prayer. I've used it here with excellent results.

When I became pregnant for the third time, I was angry! I didn't want another child: Two children were enough. I was angry with myself, with my husband, and with the unborn child. During my pregnancy I often said, "I don't want this child. I don't want to be pregnant. I don't know how I can ever love this child."

When Susan was born, my anger had cooled down a bit, and I was glad to welcome her into the family. However, the damage had been done, and I didn't realize it until years later when I heard someone tell of experimenting with hypnosis and regressing a subject back to the time in the womb. The subject could repeat conversations that the mother had had. The experimenter and subject verified this. Then I thought of all the times I'd said I didn't want Susan, and I began to wonder how I could ever undo what I'd done. I'd been using the subconscious prayer for several years and I'd been using the healing-of-the-memories prayer for some years, but suddenly I saw how I could combine the two and bring release from the past to Susan. I began using the combination, and it seemed to work. Whereas Susan had so often clung to me for reassurances of love, now she was able to make friends with others and to enjoy such things as overnight camping with girls her own age. She became independent of me, capable of directing her own life without constantly looking to me to see if I approved of what she was doing.

I've never told Susan that I used the subconscious prayer and the combination of it with the healing-of-the-memories prayer. Perhaps she'll read this book one day and learn about it. I believe that she's the delightful, free person she is today because I was led to pray in certain ways for her—ways that are quite unusual but ways which have proved to be very practical.

HEALING-OF-THE-
MEMORIES PRAYER

I first heard of the healing-of-the-memories prayer at a retreat a year after my husband's death. One of the leaders, Mignon Worley, suggested that she lead me through it. I didn't know what it was but I believed that it might help me. Mignon told me that the idea for it had first come to Agnes Sanford who'd used it with success.

After Ted died, there came to my mind so many acts of unkindness I'd done to him, and there was remorse that I hadn't done some of the things for him that I could've done so easily. These thoughts nagged at me but after the healing of the memories, the naggings never returned. I was released from the past because Jesus, who is Lord of time—past, present, and future—had released me, had cleansed and healed me. What I hadn't been able to do for myself and what others couldn't do for me by assuring me that I was forgiven, Jesus did for me one morning when Mignon led me through the steps in the healing of my memories.

Since that time, I've helped many people through this simple, beautiful prayer and into creative living, freed from past guilt and pain. I've been amazed at how parallel the lives of people are. We so often think that we alone have problems which are unique, but really we don't. All of us carry guilt and emotional scars around with us from our past. We may feel very confident that they don't influence us in the present, but if we look closely we'll discover that they are precisely what are binding us now.

I've come to the conclusion that you don't have to share your inmost hurts and guilts with any person other than Jesus. Sometimes when we confess to another person, we get little or no relief, but find ourselves almost taking pleasure in the recounting of something that's happened in the past, in hearing the "ohs" and "ahs" and "You poor thing!" from the other person. If someone wants to tell me about his past, I'm willing to listen sympathetically, but I know that I can't do anything to help that person except to take him to Jesus and let him do the healing.

A young woman came to me and poured her heart out about her fear of men. The fear had started when her father made sexual advances toward her when she was just blooming into womanhood. She'd been so shocked and frightened that she'd become afraid that every boy, every man would make such advances. She lived her teen years in terror. She had no one with whom she could share her experience, not even her mother because the father would never leave her alone with the mother.

She wanted to date, but she was afraid to do so. When she did date, the boy usually wanted to hold her hand or kiss her, and she'd never date him again. Then she met a young man who didn't even try to hold her hand. They had lots of fun together. She felt that here was a young man she could love. They were married, but she discovered she still had fear of physical contact and was very unhappy.

After she'd shared her experiences with me, I told her that Jesus could walk back in time in her life and take away the fear and shock that she'd had when her father approached her and that she'd then be able to think of the situation without pain and that she'd be free to love her husband without fear. We prayed together and Jesus did walk back in time and healed her.

The last time I saw her I asked, "How are things?" She smiled at me and said, "Things are great, really great!"

Variations of her story could be repeated a lot of times with the same result.

An older woman came to me and talked about her past. I could see that it was binding her to the extent that she was crippled emotionally and physically. I suggested that we try an experiment in prayer and pray for the healing of her memories. She'd never heard of this type of prayer, and after I explained it to her she was eager to try it, even though she didn't believe in the divinity of Jesus and was concerned that it might not work for her because of her unbelief. I assured her that this didn't make any difference at all because I'd prayed with other people who didn't but who'd been helped. I told her that I didn't understand just how Jesus did this, but I'd found that he did it and because he did, I used it. So I led her into relaxation and into visualizing Jesus in front of her looking at her with understanding and love, and then we went through the years of her life. I was aware that something was happening to her throughout the prayer. The whole time I could visualize the cleansing and healing that was taking place at each point of her life that needed healing.

When I'd finished, she sat quietly for some time, a look of peace on her lovely face, and then when she was able to speak, she said softly, "I've never had anything so meaningful before in my life." Then she went on to tell me that Jesus was very real to her during that time of prayer. I've no doubt but that that woman was healed and will be manifesting wholeness in her body.

I could have reached the woman on the mental or intellectual level. I could have used arguments which would have convinced her conscious mind that the past is past and it is better just to go on into the future, but Jesus reached her on the emotional level, and she was convinced not by what I said, but by what she experienced, that she'd been healed.

I shared with her how I'd used the prayer for the

healing of the memories with Susan because of the
emotional scars I'd left on her by my not wanting to
have another child. She asked if I'd do the same for
her children, for there were many wounds which she'd
inflicted on them. I assured her that I would and that
she could rest assured that they'd be healed.

A woman came to me at a prayer lab and said that
after the session she'd like to talk with me. I'd helped
her so much the year before with a problem she'd
faced, but now there was something else that she
needed help with. I told her I'd be glad to talk with
her. However, during that particular session, I was led
to use the healing-of-the-memories prayer with the
whole group. There were about twenty women present
that afternoon, and although I'd never used this type
of prayer with a group before, I knew that what Jesus
could do on an individual level he could do in a group.

I explained to the women what the healing of the
memories was and gave some examples of how others
had been helped by having their memories healed. I
said, "Now I've never done this with any other group,
but it's come to me that we're to pray for the healing
of the memories this afternoon. So just sit quietly and
breathe deeply and relax. Let go of tension and then
picture Jesus standing in front of you. Forget that anyone else is here and just look at Jesus and listen to me
as I lead you through this wonderful experience."

We went through the prayer slowly, visualizing each
thing as I talked. There was a sense of peace and deep
joy in the room when we finished. Many of the women
were crying very quietly, and they were tears of release and joy. It was a deeply moving experience. Some
of the women wanted to share what had happened to
them and they did. It was very beautiful. And the best
part was when the woman who'd wanted to talk with
me after the session came up to me, her face simply
glowing, and said, "I don't need to talk with you.
Everything is all right!"

You probably have need of the healing of your

memories. You may have done things in the past of which you're ashamed, or you haven't done things you wish you had. Other people may have hurt you very deeply; there's been pain or guilt or frustration or unforgiveness in your past. Well, now's the time in which you can be healed, released, and turned to the future with faith and power if you'll experiment with me.

In praying the prayer for the healing of the memories, you need to have in mind the whole sequence of the prayer so read the following suggestions carefully. Perhaps you'll want to put the prayer on a tape and use it that way, or you can have a friend lead you through it, saying the words.

Sit in a comfortable position. Breathe deeply and slowly and regularly for a while—

When you've relaxed as completely as you can, visualize Jesus standing in front of you, looking at you with love and understanding as an elder brother would who knows all about you and loves you. Let his love and understanding flow into you and rest quietly—

As I talk to him, picture what I'm saying and imagine each situation being cleansed and healed. Take your time at each point. Don't hurry. You'll probably find situations coming to your mind that you haven't thought of for years. You may feel the tears flowing, and if you do, just let them, they help in the cleansing process—

"Jesus, here is a person who needs your help, who's willing for you to walk back in time and to stop at each point of pain, each wound or scar, and bring cleansing and healing.

"Walk back, now, to the time when he (she) was a tiny embryo in his (her) mother's womb. If there were any feelings on the part of the mother or father or anyone that were negative and hurtful, cleanse those feelings. If there were hurtful words spoken, cleanse those words, take the sting out of them and let that little embryo feel and know your love cradling him (her)—

"Jesus, come in time to the birth of this person. If there was trauma and pain during the birth due to the leaving of the warmth and security of the womb and being thrust suddenly into a cold world, enfold this baby with your warmth and love and melt the shock and hurt and bring healing—

"When this person was just a small baby and child and you see that he (she) was hurt or puzzled, take that baby, that child, up into your arms and love the hurt away or unravel the puzzle and let only good be present—

"Come, Jesus, in time to this person's boyhood (girlhood) years, and wherever you see there was pain or guilt or frustration or misunderstanding, let your love flow into the situation and cleanse and heal—

"Jesus, walk into the teen years of this person's life. Nothing can escape your glance. You see everything, and you alone can take from every hurt, every fear, every frustration, every hate, the negative energy. Do that right now. Just transmute from the negative to the positive by letting your love flow into each situation the person faced and bring cleansing and healing—

"And then, Jesus, come on into the years of the twenties, and at each point where there was disappointment, failure, guilt, fear, hurt, put your arms around the person in those situations and take all the pain away and cleanse the person and let your love flow into him (her) and heal him (her)—

"Come then, Jesus, into the thirties and see each situation when this person was hurt or angered or carried guilt or felt failure, and cleanse and bless and bring healing. . .

"Come into the forties—

"Come into the fifties—

"Come into the sixties—

"Cleanse, bless, heal—

"Thank you, Jesus, for what you've done in this person, releasing him (her) from all the past which has been keeping him (her) from being a joyous, creative person. And now as you stand and look at him (her) with love and compassion, help him (her) experience your loving, healing presence right now—

"Help him (her) rest in your love, right now, experiencing the wonderful freedom which only you can give—

"And, Jesus, help this person put his (her) trust in you for the future. If there are worries and concerns about the future, help him (her) now turn them all over to you that you might bring every good and perfect gift to this person in the future. Thank you, Jesus, thank you."

As the days go by, you'll probably sense a freedom within which you haven't had for a long time or which you may never have had before. As you think about past experiences, you can happily remind yourself that Jesus has cleansed and healed them. They will cause you no pain, for he's taken the sting out of them, and you'll know they no longer bind you.

It may be that now you've experienced the healing of the memories, you'll be led to people who need the same type of prayer. You now know how to help them. Share with them how it has helped you and ask them if they'd like to try it. That's the way I did. All you have to do is help the person get to Jesus who does all the cleansing and healing.

If you believe that another person has been deeply harmed by you, you might want to go through the process of subconscious prayer, using the healing of the memories for him. But do it without telling the other person what you're doing. He never needs to know.

In order to remain cleansed and released and healed, take time each day to say something like this: "If I've been hurt in any way by anyone today, I now forgive that person. I let go of the hurt by giving it to Jesus. Take it, Jesus, cleanse it and heal me. Thank you."

If you've ever had the healing-of-the-memories

prayer, you'll see that I have adapted it into what is for me the most meaningful way. I always experiment with prayer until I come up with the best way for me. I suggest that you do the same thing. Just because someone has used it in a certain way for a long period of time doesn't mean that will be the most meaningful way for you. From their particular form of praying, you can add variations which have special meaning for you.

Remember the story about the holy man in India who was bothered by mice playing around him when he meditated? He got a cat and tied it to a stake near him so that the mice would be scared away. He never explained to his disciples why he had a cat staked out in his meditation room, but when they meditated, they thought they had to have a cat staked out beside them.

There is no magic in any form or ritual that I know of, but there is power in whatever holds meaning for you. Experiment until you find what is meaningful.

LAYING-ON-OF-HANDS PRAYER

In the prayer labs and workshops I conduct, the culmination of our time together has come to be the "glory seat." The idea for the glory seat came to me at the first national retreat of Spiritual Frontiers Fellowship several years ago.

My prayer group was meeting outdoors under tall trees. We sat on little stools, benches, and chairs. I took one of the stools without a back and set it in the center of our circle and said, "This is the glory seat. Any one of you who wants to can come sit on it, and the rest of us'll lay our hands on you, and God'll pour his glory through us to you to bless you and to meet your every need." The glory seat proved to be such a blessing that week that when I began leading prayer workshops and labs throughout the country, I always had the glory seat as a part of our final session. Something happens when a group of people make themselves available for God to pour himself through to bless another person. Those who lay hands on another experience it, and the person who receives the laying on of hands experiences it.

I want to share with you some experiences in laying on hands so that you can see the many different things that can happen when an individual or a group makes itself available for God to pour his blessings through.

At one retreat I led, I was showing the group the

mechanics for the laying on hands. I asked for a volunteer to be our "patient," and a woman came forward. She sat in a chair in the center of our circle. I
said, "Relax, each one of you and become receptive to
God. Just breathe deeply and evenly and let go of
tension. We'll take time to prepare ourselves to become
channels for God to pour himself through." I suggested
to the woman in the chair that she breathe deeply, too,
and that she relax as much as possible and hold a receptive attitude. When it seemed that there was a feeling of relaxation present, I said, "Now we'll hold this
same feeling and very quietly get up and walk over to
the glory seat and lay our hands on our patient. If you
can't touch her comfortably, just touch someone who's
touching her," and we moved over quietly, laying our
hands on her, maintaining an attitude of relaxation and
receptivity. Then I said, "Now, hold the picture of
yourself as a tube which lets the love and power and
healing and glory of God just pour through it. Don't
think about anything but that you're letting God flow
through you."

There seemed to be a heightening of power in the
room as we stood with our hands on the woman. Then
I said, "Thank you, Father, that you've used us as
channels to pour your healing and blessing and glory
through to your daughter. Thank you," and all the
people said, "Amen, amen, amen." The rest of the
group joined in on the amens.

We moved quietly back to our places and the woman
got up and walked to her chair in the corner. We continued the workshop with another woman sharing with
us a technique of healing. During her sharing, the
"patient" came up to me and said, "I think I've been
healed." I turned to look at her, and I saw tears in her
eyes. "I've had bursitis in my arm so badly that I
couldn't raise it to my shoulder, but look," and she
lifted her arm up into the air and began to rotate it.
We two just stood there, thanking God for what he'd
done. Then, when the demonstration was over, we

shared with the group what had happened and spent some time in rejoicing.

At one of the prayer workshops, the minister of the church had been in a car accident the week before and had received a whiplash. He'd been under a doctor's care. He sat in the glory seat and literally felt the pulsating power of God flowing through us and was healed. His whole ministry's changed. He's begun talking to his congregation about personally experiencing God and his power and the need to balance love for humanity with love for God. Many people in his church are experiencing God.

My daughter, Susan, once came into my room where I was working at my typewriter and said that she had a tummyache. I had her lie down on my bed and I laid my hands on her tummy and visualized that I was just a channel for God to pour himself through to her. I sat quietly for a while. Soon she said, "I think I'll go watch television," and she got up and left. Later though, she came back into my room and said, "Mommy, what did you do to take the tummyache away?" I said, "Why, I just imagined that I was a tube through which God was flowing into you to make you OK." "Oh," she said and left the room.

A minister I know has a number of prayer groups in his church. One group began experimenting with the laying on of hands. They decided to make individual experiments in which each one would quietly put his hands on a beloved person while that person slept, and would just offer himself as a channel for God to pour through to bless the person. They wouldn't tell God what to do, they'd just be channels for whatever he wanted to do.

One woman later reported that her husband worked in a job that was very demanding of his eyes. He began going blind and the doctor assured him that he'd need to learn Braille because he'd eventually be completely blind. The woman began to lay her hands on her husband after he was asleep and saw herself as a channel for God to bless him. Several weeks went by, and then the man was examined by his doctor, who examined him not only once, but twice. He finally told the man that the first diagnosis had been wrong, that the man's eyes were improving and that there was no need for him to continue learning Braille.

The woman brought the good news to the prayer group. Because she'd felt that the husband wouldn't be sympathetic with what she'd done, she never told him of laying her hands on him each night and being a channel for God to bless him. She is convinced that the diagnosis had been correct and that God had worked a miracle through the laying on of hands.

On my first trip to India I ate the local food and drank the local water wherever I went. But when I was in New Delhi a few days before my departure for the States, I had a severe case of diarrhea. That night after I'd tucked in the mosquito netting around my bed, I laid my hands on my stomach and imagined that God was flowing through my hands to heal me. I fell asleep and when I awakened in the morning, I was well.

One night a friend and I took the night shift from eleven to seven with a high school girl who'd been in a car accident. When we arrived at the hospital I saw the poor girl in a bed that had the sides raised on it. She looked like an animal in a cage. Her head had been shaved and a little stubble had grown out on it. She was writhing all over the bed because of gas pains. I don't know why I did what I did, but I walked directly over to her, put my hands through the bars, laid them on her stomach and said, "Take the pain and the cause of the pain away in the Name of Jesus." Her legs straightened out, she settled into a comfortable position and fell asleep and slept the whole night through.

A woman I know was going to be interviewed on a television program. She had been used often as a channel through which God poured his healing. As she and the interviewer walked down the hall together to the studio, she lovingly put her hands on the other woman's back. After the program, the interviewer told her that she'd been having trouble with her back, but when my friend put her hand on it as they walked down the hall, the pain had just disappeared and she felt just fine.

Another woman called me one day to say that she'd discovered a lump in her breast. She asked me to pray for her, so right then on the phone I prayed aloud. When she came early to the prayer group a day or so later, she asked if I'd pray again and have the laying on of hands. I laid my hands on her and saw myself as a channel through which God was pouring healing. She and I both felt a warmth in my hands and a heightened awareness of God's presence with us.

She called me a few days later to rejoice with me. The lump had begun diminishing in size immediately and was now completely gone. She said she'd had a lump about a year before which hadn't gone away, and after two weeks she'd gone to a doctor. He found that it was benign and had aspirated it. She felt our prayers this time and particularly the laying-on-of-hands prayer had allowed God to flow into her and heal her.

I met a man at a retreat who was deaf in his right ear. He explained that he'd had an operation quite a long time ago and that part of his ear had been removed. I got the feeling that I should pray for the man, but I felt foolish at the thought of asking him for he'd explained that the operation had made it impossible for him to hear. Yet the feeling was so strong within me that I finally asked if he'd mind if I prayed for him. He smiled indulgently and said, "You may pray for me, but it won't do any good." I rounded up three friends who believed in the power of prayer, and we took the man outside the auditorium. We had him sit on the runningboard of an old car that was in the parking lot. I put my index fingers in his ears; Barbara stood to the man's right, one hand on him and one on me; Jean stood behind me with her hands on my shoulders, and Jack stood behind her with his hands on her shoulders. I began to pray aloud, "Oh, thank you, Lord——" but that was as far as I got. Suddenly the air became charged with power. Something powerful hit Jack in his back, passed through him to Jean, hit her and passed through her to me, and passed through me into that man's ear. We all began to thank God. The man asked if he could try to listen to my watch. He could hear the ticking with the ear that had been deaf. The next morning when I saw him, he literally shone with joy. He could still hear out of the ear. Several months later I had a letter from him saying that he was now being used as a channel to heal others.

I have one friend who's a channel of healing for me. She isn't aware that healing is flowing through us and can hardly believe her eyes when I'm healed, but if I have an ache or pain anywhere, I just ask her to lay her hands on me and I'm well. It's so easy to picture God's healing flowing through her to me.

A woman's daughter-in-law was expecting her first child and was in her eighth month of pregnancy. She'd been extremely well, but one day she noticed a bad taste in her mouth. Her left eye watered and her mouth drooped on the left side. Several days before she'd had some dental work done and thought it might be a reaction to the novocaine. When she talked with her dentist, he assured her that this couldn't be and suggested that she see her obstetrician. Within a few days, her face on the left side had become paralyzed. The eyelid drooped, the mouth was contorted, and she had difficulty in speaking and swallowing. She consulted her doctor who said that the paralysis involved the seventh facial muscle. At first he minimized the seriousness of her condition, saying that it might last several months or longer and asked her to see a specialist. The only medication he prescribed at that time was vitamin B. Later he referred to her condition as Bell's Palsy and indicated that she was thoroughly afflicted.

The woman was in despair for her daughter-in-law. She kept her constantly in her thoughts and prayers.

Then one day I was visiting in her city and happened to be where she worked. She had previously attended a prayer retreat I'd led and so she knew me. When she saw me, she immediately asked if she could talk with me, and we found a quiet room. She told me what had happened with her daughter-in-law and asked me to pray for her. I asked her if she would sit as proxy for her daughter-in-law while I laid my hands on her and prayed. I stood behind her and placed my hands on her face. She told me later that my hands became very warm and the heat from them penetrated her face. I stood seeing myself as a channel for God to pour his healing through. Somehow I was aware that something was happening. The woman later told me that in a few minutes she was aware of a great sense of relief and was filled with a sense of serenity and with the assurance that something good had happened.

I thanked God that he'd poured through me to heal the young woman, gave the mother-in-law a hug, and went on my way.

Several weeks later I had a phone call from the woman. Her daughter-in-law had finally seen the specialist who'd been advised of the extent of the facial damage and the seriousness of the young woman's condition. When he examined her, these are the words he used, "This is a miracle. I've never seen any person with Bell's Palsy recover this quickly." His examination showed that she was on the road to recovery with only 3 percent paralysis left in her face.

Her face had begun to improve from the time we'd prayed for her. She even told her mother-in-law that a strange thing happened to her at that time. Her face had tingled, and that was the first time she'd had any sensation since she'd been afflicted. Only later did the woman tell her that we'd prayed for her. The incident ends with a complete recovery for the young woman.

In the prayer labs and workshops we often stand in a circle and face to the right, laying our hands on the shoulders of the person now in front of us. We thank

God for that person and visualize ourselves as channels through which God is pouring blessings to that person. We stay in this attitude for a while, and then we turn around and place our hands on the shoulders of the person who had been behind us, blessing us, and we let God's blessings pour into that person.

Other times, while we're sitting we imagine that the power of God is flowing around our circle, first to the right, and we visualize it flowing through our hands, going around the circle until it comes back to us, then flowing out and around through the circle again and again. We then visualize it flowing to the left, going around the circle and back, out again and back, and out a third time and back. When it returns the third time, we visualize the love and blessing and power of God in us.

I was asked to lead a prayer group at a one-day Ashram and used the touching or linking of hands and the visualizing of the power of God flowing around our circle. Several weeks later I was at another meeting, and a woman came up to me and introduced herself. She said, "I was in your prayer group at the Ashram. I'd had sinus trouble so badly that I hadn't planned to attend the Ashram that day, but I thought I might as well be miserable there as at home. You know, when we joined hands in our circle my sinuses cleared up, and I've had no problem with them since then."

I believe every contact we make with our hands can be a contact for blessing. Every time we're introduced to someone we can think as we're shaking hands, "Thanks, Father, for flowing through me to bless this person." Every time we lay a hand on the shoulder of a friend, we can think, "Thanks, Father, for blessing this friend through me." Every time we are touched by another, we can think, "Thanks, Father, for blessing me through this person." Touching, then, takes on a holiness.

Begin to open yourself to God to let him flow through. Be aware of his power flowing out from your hands. If you can't feel it, then picture it streaming out, and send it to people you know who are in need of love or healing or blessing.

As you work with your hands, see the love and blessing of God going into your work. Remind yourself often as you use your hands that each person or thing you touch is being blessed because God flows through you. As you do this, God has an open channel through which to pour his blessing and glory. The point of contact between him and another can be your hands.

LISTENING PRAYER

In our culture where we're busily involved from early morning to late night, it isn't easy for us to relax and become receptive to God. We'd much rather make a list of what we need to do that day, rush to an empty chair, sit on the edge of it and say, "Father, I need your help," hold the list up for a divine stamp of approval and then rush off, never thinking of God again that day.

In listening prayer we must learn to quiet our bodies and our minds and put ourselves in a receptive attitude, an attitude of waiting, of listening.

We live in a world of noises. We've become so accustomed to some of the noises that we're unaware of them until we sit down to settle into silence, then we hear the construction crew down the block, an airplane overhead, the dryer, the children laughing, a dog barking, ad infinitum.

When you've decided to take time to become quiet and to relax, deal with the noises bothering you. If you can turn off the dryer for a while, good. You can't stop the construction crew down the block or the airplane overhead, so bless them. You can say, "I bless the construction crew. The men are strong and healthy and are earning a living for their families. I'm glad they have work." You can say, "Bless the plane and everyone on it. Uphold it with your love, Father."

If you let noises upset you, your ear stays open to them. When you bless them, the ear tunes them down or out.

After dealing with noises, you'll probably find all sorts of thoughts coming into your mind. I've discovered that thoughts are like children; ignore them and they come back again and again; listen to them and they will go away.

My daughter, Susan, used to come pull on my skirt when I was busy preparing a meal, grading papers, or working on an article which had to be in by a certain deadline. If I'd ignore her, she'd be persistent; however if I put down whatever I was doing, looked her straight in the eye and listened, then make an appropriate remark, she'd run off happy as could be. When I learned to take thoughts that came to me during listening time, listen to them, then spiritualize them, my listening time turned into a joy rather than a struggle.

For instance, I'd gone to the college chapel lounge to meet with the student prayer group one morning from six-thirty to seven. I'd finished my packing for the trip I was to take back East, and after the prayer group meeting, I'd pick up my bag and go to the airport. As I sat quietly, breathing deeply and relaxing, it suddenly popped into my mind that I hadn't put out the garbage, and it was pickup day. I immediately spiritualized the thought, "Oh, Father, lift out all the garbage in my life." I imagined that just as I'd lift the sacks of garbage out of the containers, God lifted sacks of garbage out of me. I thanked him and waited in silence. Then I thought, "I forgot to water the plants," and I said, "Father, I'm like parched ground. Water me with your Holy Spirit," and I imagined a gentle rain of God's Spirit coming down on me. I then slipped into an awareness of God's presence and joined the others in the group in praying for friends and concerns.

At seven o'clock I went home, set out the garbage, and watered the house plants. I was glad the thoughts concerning them had come to me. I think God was speaking to me in the thoughts because he wanted me to take care of my responsibilities at home as well as travel many miles to lead a prayer lab.

God is speaking all the time, all the time, all the time, as Frank Laubach has said. I believe he is, but we need to learn to recognize his voice. We need to tune our ears to God's wavelength, and just as a radio has to be delicately adjusted, to get the fine tuning we want, so our ears must be carefully tuned, to hear the voice of God. One way to hear God's voice is by reading some devotional book or the Bible.

Once at a prayer lab a woman said, "God never speaks to me at all."

"Do you read your Bible?" I asked her.

"Well," she replied hesitantly, "no, I don't read it." Then I told the story of Howard.

I was at a church board meeting one night and made what I thought was a clever, cutting remark to Howard, one of the board members. I slept well that night, quite pleased with myself for being so witty and incisive. The next morning when I was having my listening time, I was reading from Matthew 5:23:24. "If, when you are bringing your gift to the altar, you suddenly remember that your brother has a grievance against you, leave your gift where it is before the altar. First go and make your peace with your brother, and only then come back and offer your gift (NEB)." I was going to read on, but my eyes went back again to those verses, and I reread them. "OK, OK," I thought, "I understand," but my eyes returned to the verses again and I reread them. It dawned on me that God was talking to me about Howard. Howard had a grievance against me. I knew I was to go and apologize to him, but I didn't want to at all. I tried to think of every reason why I shouldn't go. The best reason seemed to be that the car probably wouldn't start. It was a cold morning, and often on cold mornings the car just wouldn't start. But I seemed to hear a voice say, "Why don't you try it, anyway?" I slipped into my coat, got the car key, went out the kitchen door into the garage, got into the car, put the key in, turned it on, and the motor roared to life. Reluctantly I got out, opened the garage door, got back in, backed out, wheeled around, and headed down the dirt road to the highway, thinking, "There's that bad curve on the way to Howard's. I'll probably hit loose gravel and land in the ditch." I was almost anticipating the curve, the loose gravel and the ditch when I turned off the highway and onto the graveled road. I sailed past the bad curve without a hitch and thought, "Maybe Howard's finished the milking and he's gone into town already," but when I pulled into the lane, I saw the milking parlor lights on. Oh, how I wanted to swing the car around and head home, but I didn't. Somehow, I kept going. I stopped the car and sat trying to figure out how I could apologize to Howard without seeming like a fool. I'd go in, walk up to him, shake his hand, and say, "Howard, I want to apologize for saying what I did last night. I know I hurt you by saying it. I'm sorry," and I'd turn around and walk out.

Well, I got out of the car and walked to the door of the milking parlor. As I opened the door the smell of warm milk mingled with manure hit me. I was nauseated and I wanted to run, but Howard saw me. He came toward me, smelly and rough in his work clothes, and suddenly what I'd planned to say was forgotten. I was miserable that I had hurt this good man. I blurted out, "Howard, I'm so sorry for what I said last night. I'm sorry I hurt you. Will you forgive me?" and I started to cry. I saw his face crumple, too, and we ran to each other. There we stood, our arms around each other, my head buried in his chest, and there in that smelly old milking parlor we experienced the forgiveness and love of each other and God. Finally I lifted my head, and Howard and I smiled at each other through our tears. A healing had taken place in a few minutes, and we were at peace with each other.

The car seemed to fly home on wings of joy and

praise. I wondered how I could ever have felt I didn't want to go see Howard and apologize. I got home, took off my coat, walked over to the easy chair, sat down, picked up my Bible, then closed my eyes and said, "Father, I fought it all the way, but I did what you said. I made peace with my brother, and I'm glad, really glad, that you made me do it. Thank you, thank you!"

God speaks to us through his Word, often very pointedly as he did with me about Howard, but at other times he speaks to assure us that he's leading and helping us.

When we lived in Madagascar and Ted was working for Church World Service, he and I started reading the Psalms aloud after we were in bed at night. Ted went on a trip to the eastern coast, and I read a psalm aloud each night. Ted was killed on that trip, when the single engine plane he and three other men were in crashed into a mountain. But I didn't learn about his death until four days after it happened. When he didn't return home as expected, I asked a friend, who was a pilot, to call the airport for me to see what radio communication there had been. He reported that the men had radioed they were leaving Maroansetra that morning and would fly to Nossi-Bé. There was no word the next day, but the following day I learned that the plane had never reached its destination. The American Embassy plane, the French Embassy plane, and several Aero-club planes were dispatched to scour the countryside. During the period of waiting for news, there was within me a feeling of great strength and power. I knew that wherever Ted was, he was in God's Hands. Word finally came that the plane had been found and that all had died in the crash. That strength and power within stayed strong and steady. Ted and I had often talked of life after death and both felt that at death one moves into an expanded life, a new dimension, into one of the many mansions Jesus talked about before his death.

That night after the news came that Ted was dead, I

went to bed and picked up the Bible. I didn't know just what my daughters and I would do, but I felt we had to return to the States. I opened the Bible to the Thirty-second Psalm. My eyes were immediately fixed on the eighth verse, "I will instruct you and teach you the way you should go." I closed my eyes and thanked God for his words of assurance to me.

About a week later, I went through Ted's papers. He wrote a great deal. He'd done quite a lot of photo-journalism. He wrote, from time to time, as though he were an older pastor, advising a younger one named Tom on some problem. Out of a stack of papers a foot and a half high, I just happened to pull one sheet of paper. It was a letter to Tom suggesting what he should say to a young widow whose husband had died very suddenly. I suppose I'll always remember one of the sentences that leaped out at me. "Certainly God didn't cause this tragedy, but God can use it for good." I knew that God was speaking to me, that I had been led to pull that particular sheet out of the stack. Tears of joy slipped down my cheeks and I murmured over and over, "Thank you, thank you."

God speaks to us today if we have ears to hear, and one beautiful way he speaks is through other people.

Often after a prayer lab, a person will come up to me and ask if I'd been "picking up" his particular need because what I'd said had spoken directly to him. I have to admit that I hadn't directly "picked up" his need but I had tried to stay open to the Holy Spirit of God so that he could minister to anyone who needed him. Apparently the Holy Spirit had known his need and had met it.

God often speaks through people in a prayer group. For instance, the group grows quiet and waits in the silence. As thoughts come to various ones, these are shared. The sharing may be a verse of Scripture, a line from a hymn, or a song someone starts and the rest join in on. Those in the group find God speaking to them and ministering to them through the others in the group.

One time God spoke directly and pointedly to me through a woman who was teaching a class at the Church of the Brethren Seminary in Chicago. We had moved to Chicago after a term of service for the church in Iraq. Our first daughter, Fran, was just a baby. Ted took a full schedule of classes and also worked eight hours a day. I didn't have the opportunity to take any classes, but I did sit in on a class for ministers' wives called The Devotional Life whenever I could. This particular night, I was filled with joy because the teacher, Anna Mow, was thrilling me with what she was saying. I guess I was sitting in the seat smiling and nodding my head as she talked as I often do when I agree with people. Suddenly Anna stopped what she was saying and looked at me. "What are you nodding your head for; you don't know what I'm talking about." She must have carried on the class, I don't remember. I only knew that I had never been so humiliated in my whole life. I prayed that the floor would open up and swallow me. As soon as class was over, I slipped out a nearby door and went home and cried.

Then I got mad. "Just who does she think she is that she can humiliate me? She doesn't have any idea of all the experiences with God I've had." I looked at myself and felt that I was as perfect as a human could be. I really didn't have any faults. That poor woman just didn't know what she was talking about. I'd show her. I'd pray that God would reveal my faults to me if I had any and when he didn't reveal any to me, I'd go to her and tell her.

Well, I flippantly prayed that God would reveal my faults to me, and as the days went by he began to show me just what I was really like. It was awful. One after another fault was shown me, and I got to the point that I couldn't stand to look at myself in the mirror. I couldn't keep food down. I was miserable for days and days. Finally I had sense enough to go talk with Anna

Mow and tell her how I had reacted to her humiliating me and also tell her how very grateful I now was because I was seeing myself as I really was. Her answer was, "We don't see the dust until the light is turned on." Then she prayed with me, asking God to help make me into the person he wanted me to be, and I was able to look at myself again, knowing that he was at work in me. As painful as the whole experience was, I'm glad for it, and I feel sure that God was speaking to me through Anna. I do recommend, though, that if you ever ask God to reveal your faults to you, that you add, "Just one at a time, please."

Sometimes in waiting quietly in God's presence, pictures come to mind, and words and thoughts. It's good to have pencil and paper available so that you can jot these pictures and thoughts down. God speaks to us through our imaginings and thoughts, and it's always wise to ask for an interpretation. I know that the first time a picture came to me, I didn't know what it meant. I was a college girl. I was attending a retreat and was a part of a prayer group. A woman in the group had asked for prayer for her mother, but she hadn't said what was wrong with her mother. I closed my eyes, and immediately I saw with my inner eye myself carrying a woman in my arms up some marble steps. At the top of the steps, Jesus stood. I laid the woman down at his feet. She sat up and began to sing. After the prayer group, I talked with the woman. Her mother was partially paralyzed in the throat. Her doctor had recommended that she sing a lot as therapy.

I learned as more and more of these pictures came to me to ask, "Father, what does this mean?" Not always, but most of the time, an interpretation came to me.

If the pictures or thoughts involve someone else, ask God if you are to share what came with that person. Pray the increase-decrease prayer about this, and if the desire to share with them increases, then do so. Often you won't understand what you see or hear, but the other person you share it with will. But be careful that you don't get guidance for other people. They are responsible to get their own guidance. As long as you act as a mediator for them, they won't deepen their own relationship with God, or at least, they're less likely to do so.

Sometimes during listening prayer ideas flow readily, and you write them down. When you finish you discover that you have some beautiful, helpful thoughts that seem not only to apply to you but seem to have a universal application. This is wonderful, and you may be led to share what comes through with others who will be blessed also by what you receive. There is a caution here, however, that I feel I must make. There may be times when the pencil you use seems to take on a life of its own and write and write and write. This is known as automatic handwriting, and it can be extremely dangerous. Always go into a time of listening prayer asking the protection and love of Jesus to surround you because if you don't, you leave yourself wide open to any spirit that may be around, and what you want is the Holy Spirit of God to come to you.

I have worked with several people who have done automatic writing. The pattern has always been the same. The messages are beautiful, inspiring, helpful to begin with. Later they begin subtly to change in tone until the messages become ugly. When the writer tries to stop writing, he begins to hear sounds day and night and feels prickles on the body. He becomes extremely upset emotionally, thinking he's going insane. Only months of working with a person like this brings release. Then the person can never go back to writing. My advice is this: Leave automatic writing alone, even though you've received wonderful messages so far. The pattern just hasn't been completely laid out yet, you just haven't moved into the second, third, and fourth stages. The hell you will go through is not worth what you're receiving now.

My advice may seem extreme, but I have seen too

many people who've become involved in this stage of listening who couldn't handle what happened. Keep your eyes on Jesus. Bring everything to him. He can handle anything. There's always more good unfolding as you follow him, so don't let yourself be sidetracked.

Also, if you begin to see with your inner eye people who talk directly to you, always ask if the spirit comes in the Name of Jesus. You know, we're told in I John 4:1-3, "Don't trust every spirit, dear friends of mine, but test them to discover whether they come from God or not. . . . You can test them in this simple way: every spirit that acknowledges the fact that Jesus, God's Christ, actually became man, comes from God, but the spirit which denies this fact does not come from God (Phillips)."

If you can get help from the highest level, God, Jesus, the Holy Spirit, why settle for anything less?

There is always the possibility that we become satisfied too early in our listening prayer. We are so pleased with what comes to us in the listening that we would simply stay there forever. Usually, however, we have enough sense to realize that what we need from our listening is strength and power to live our everyday, workaday lives in a creative, triumphant way.

It's wonderful to have a quiet time daily, to pull off into a secluded place and be alone and have experiences, but if that quiet time and the experiences don't enable you to meet your responsibilities in your work and your home, of what value are they really? It's so easy to delude ourselves that we are becoming spiritual because we have a daily quiet time and some experiences. But how well do you get along with your colleagues, your family, your friends? You bring glory to God when you're involved in daily life, trying to let his love flow through you in each situation and to each person.

Daily quiet time used to be so important to me that I would yell at my children in "righteous indignation" when they wouldn't be still so I could have my quiet time. Then it would take me a long time to settle down into the silence because of the turmoil within created when I got upset with them. I finally realized that letting love flow through me to my children was more important than having a little experience in some quiet corner. So I arranged to have my quiet time either when the children were in bed or outside playing. I became a much more loving mother.

We've talked about many levels of listening prayer, but there is a level of listening prayer which goes far beyond anything we've talked about so far. At this level you are aware that God pours himself into and around and through you in a holy quietness which is healing to your body and mind and spirit. There is no feeling of separation. There is only a feeling and knowing of oneness or at-one-ment with him. You realize with quiet joy that he is yours and you are his.

This is the beginning of the ultimate glory of prayer. At last you experience what God would have you experience all the time.

THE ULTIMATE GLORY
OF PRAYER

All that we've shared so far has been shared to help you get to the point where God, manifesting as Father, Son, or Holy Spirit, can break through to you and become infused in you and then live through you. For the ultimate glory of prayer is this—letting God live through you in every circumstance and with every person.

Very few of us are taught the truth that we're to live our lives in union with God, with Jesus. We've somehow taken the words, "I am the vine, you are the branches, . . . apart from me you can do nothing" (John 15:5), that Jesus spoke the night before he died, and we've seen them as beautiful literature but not really as the last great lesson he taught his disciples. But the disciples soon learned, didn't they, that his words weren't just beauty-filled, they were also reality? For when the Holy Spirit that Jesus promised them came and infused them with power, they began to become like Jesus and to do the things he'd done. The very life of power and healing which flowed through him, flowed through them. And a later disciple, Paul, was even known to have cried, "It isn't I who lives, but Christ in me!"

What a far cry from that which he uttered earlier, when he said he was wretched because he did the very things he didn't want to do and left undone the things he did want to do. Surely he went through a growing, learning process until he experienced the oneness, the union of his life with that of Christ Jesus. And we, too, must go through a growing, learning process before we come to union, the ultimate glory of prayer.

Many of us are so geared to instant potatoes, instant cement, instant service, and instant this, that, and the other, that we think we can have instant union with God.

We're very much like one of my daughters who wants to be a singer but who won't go through the disciplines which will give her control of her voice. She wants instant success in singing. As far as I know, she'll never have it. What she has at the present is a good voice, but she doesn't control it; therefore, really, it's useless, for it won't do what she wants it to do. But if she'll learn to control it by accepting and practicing the disciplines which her singing teacher is trying to teach her, the sky's the limit.

If you want to come into a life of power and peace, joy and creativity, and a life of union where all that's in the Vine can flow through you, there are certain disciplines which must be accepted and practiced. Relaxation is essential. Visualization is essential. Relinquishment is essential. Praying for others in many different ways is essential. Listening is essential.

There was a time when I spent three hours in prayer every day, one hour in the morning, one hour after lunch, and one hour before I went to bed. I read, I prayed, I was immersed in the consciousness of God's presence during those hours. Everything I did in the way of discipline was like putting money into a bank. As I needed to draw strength or inner peace or power or whatever, it was there for me to draw from. And there came a day when I badly needed to draw from it, and there it was, treasure I'd stored years and months and days before, ready to pour into me to meet my need.

Since that time, I've been kept in an almost constant

state of union with God, with Jesus, which is unbelievable to most people who haven't experienced it themselves but which is understood by those who've experienced it. And I believe that it could never have happened to me if I hadn't had years of discipline in the area of prayer.

I had a foretaste of the glory of union at the time of my husband's death. When I was told that his plane was missing, I knew the power and peace and presence of God immediately. There was no having to turn in prayer to him and ask for help. He was there. And during those days of waiting, I experienced an inner strength that I wouldn't have dreamed of earlier in my life. It was powerful, sustaining. I experienced angels ministering to me, succoring me. This was something I wouldn't have believed possible. Later when I learned that the plane had crashed and burned and all in it had died, the strength and power and presence only intensified. I knew in the depths of me what Jesus meant when he said, "I am with you always." His presence within me was an almost constant reality as the days passed.

A missionary friend, in whom I confided concerning the power and presence of God, told me that the strength was given me so that the shock of Ted's death wouldn't be more than I could stand, but that I wasn't to be disappointed when it left, for it couldn't remain. I'd eventually feel the letdown and I'd have to resume normal life.

Today I carry with me the sense of presence and strength and power. Rather than its lessening with the days and weeks and months and years, it's increased, and I've come to the conclusion that this is really the normal way to live and what I'd known before was a subnormal way to live. Because I hadn't known any better, I'd thought that the way I was living was normal. But I now know a state of being in which all tragedy, all suffering, all impatience, all anger—before they become those things—are turned into triumphant, creative living.

In the subnormal state I'd called on God, on Jesus, as a separate, outside being, but after an experience of knowing union with God, I know that he's within, always has been and always will be, totally identified with me as me.

Shortly after we'd returned to the States following Ted's death, my daughters and I attended a prayer retreat in Ohio. We'd talked all week about Jesus being the same yesterday, today, and forever and how he heals today. We drove to North Manchester, Indiana, where I was to teach in the fall, to choose a home for the coming school year. We stayed overnight in a girls' dorm on the campus. Fran and I slept in one room and Susan and Kay in the one next door.

During the night, I was awakened by something. I listened and then realized that someone next door was whimpering. I ran to the girls' room and there was Susan in a heap on the floor, whimpering pitiably. She'd fallen from the top bunk, had hit the big, heavy door on the way down and lay in a pool of blood on the floor, I scooped her up and took her across the hall to the bathroom. I set her on her feet and examined her. Her nose was bleeding and there was blood coming from her mouth. Usually I stop a nosebleed by pressing the nostrils together, but when I tried this, the blood backed up and caused Susan to choke. I knew I couldn't help her. It flashed into my mind that at the retreat we'd talked about Jesus' power to heal today. I knew that he alone could help her. I turned and left her. I walked to my room and picked up a washcloth and towel, knowing within that Jesus was healing Susan. When I returned to the bathroom, the bleeding had stopped, and I thankfully dampened the washcloth, slipped Susan's nightie off, and began to clean her face and body.

I think that if I were the most gifted poetess alive, I'd be unable to find words to describe what I next experienced as I washed Susan. It was as though the whole world around me were alight with all the beauty and glory of a magnificent sunrise. It was as though I could see the far reaches of land and sea and sky, and I was a part of it all. The realization came to me that God and I were one, that we always had been and we always would be. It was as though time were suspended and past, present, and future merged into a sense of continuity, of eternity. There was no separation but a reality of the immediate now which always had been and always would be. The sense of oneness is indescribable. You who've experienced it know, without my having to try to find an analogy, what I mean. You who don't understand can yet experience it. It is complete union with everything, past, present, future.

Sometimes today, I become so aware of this union that I want to fall on my knees in praise and thanksgiving and at the same time stand tall and straight and power-filled. Even now, as I write these words, such a wave of joy wells up within and washes over me from without, that the ecstasy is almost more than I can bear and I wait for it to subside, to grow gentler, until I can endure it.

Since that initial experience, this sense of union, support, power is almost continually with me. I seem to have an inveterate optimism about everything. It isn't, I believe, a sickening pollyannaism, but a way of seeing what is to be seen of pain and suffering and grimness, yet going beyond it to Reality which swallows up and transmutes the outer into peace and patience and power within.

Let me assure you that what I've tried to express so inadequately has been experienced by many people throughout the ages. It isn't just a lot of empty talk; it's a reality which I believe we're meant to experience, everyone of us.

I've talked with many people who feel their lives must be relevant to the world we live in. I couldn't agree with them more. A life of discipline and prayer can be lived in the midst of a busy schedule. It doesn't have to be accompanied by a withdrawal from the world. Some people have the erroneous idea that to lead a life of prayer you must withdraw and stay withdrawn from the world. Have you read the life of Jesus? Have you read the lives of the saints? Haven't you seen that their lives were relevant? You may be called to take several hours each day, as I was, to immerse yourself in God, in Jesus, or you may find that you need a week or more at a retreat where you can spend that time listening to God, to Jesus. But I believe that you're needed in the world, and you'll only be called to that which will fit you the best in your particular situation.

One woman I know made arrangements to have her family cared for while she spent almost a month in study and quiet and prayer. Another person I know sets his alarm for five o'clock so that he can have time alone before the rest of the family awakens. You'll be led, and you'll find that in the very midst of the pressures of life, in the middle of pain and suffering, how to become more than conqueror through an inward feeding of your mind and spirit on Jesus, taking the life which flows through the Vine and living on it.

I knew a man, a psychiatrist from another country, who'd induced the union experience with a hallucinogenic drug. What he wanted to know from me was how to sustain the experience. I had to tell him that there are no short cuts. Discipline in prayer is the prerequisite. Learning how to relax, to clear the channel, then to make ourselves available to God to be used or not used in whatever way he wants, can bring us to the point of readiness for union which is sustained.

Martha, in the New Testament, fretted and stewed around, trying to do things for Jesus, but Mary sat at his feet and learned from him. He said that Mary had chosen the better part, to be teachable. But the great thing is that when we do discipline ourselves in prayer, it isn't long before it's possible to talk, to work, to do anything, and yet inwardly be listening to and praising God.

So be patient with yourself and your spiritual growth. As the farmer tills the soil, plants the best seeds he can buy and waters and cultivates until the harvest comes, so you, by living a disciplined prayer life can prepare for the harvest, the ultimate glory of prayer, union.

The farmer doesn't go around bemoaning that he doesn't yet have his harvest when his plants are at the shoot stage or the blossom stage, but he's grateful for the present stage of growth, and he holds anticipation in his heart for what's to come. You too, rather than bemoaning, can begin to be grateful for the stage of growth you're in now, anticipating the harvest of union which will inevitably come, the fruit which will bless many.

The quickest way to speed the process of growth along is revealed by Paul, "In all things give thanks." For when you begin to make your attitude one of gratitude and thanksgiving, your spiritual life receives an infusion of power which thrusts the growth forward. Even though your first reaction to something may be despair or disappointment or a giving in to pain, make your action of thanksgiving and gratitude immediately. "I don't see how in the world, Father, you can bring good out of this, but I thank you that that's exactly what you're doing, whether I see it now or not. Thanks for being in charge and for letting your perfect will be done. Thank you."

I don't know how many times I've said such a prayer, even when I didn't feel like saying it, even when I felt nothing good could come. But determined to voice gratitude, I've said such a prayer aloud or silently and I've watched in amazement how God worked through the situation to bring good to all concerned. My gratitude, even grudgingly given, was a channel through which God was able to flow to work his wonders. Turning your eyes on Jesus, on God, and thanking him somehow opens the gate within for joy and love to flow in. Whereas centering on the problem or anything else, no matter how good it may be, closes the gate within and joy and love can't flow.

I've talked with many people who've had some absolutely marvelous spiritual experiences but who've become so enamored with the experiences that they don't manifest joy and love, two of the prime evidences of the Spirit of God at work in a person.

A woman I know had come into an experience in the baptism of the Holy Spirit where she spoke in tongues, yet there was fear and unforgiveness in her and little evidence of a flowing joy and love. She needed help and knew it. Because I speak in tongues, she was willing to listen to what I had to say about her need to grow spiritually. She'd become so enthused about speaking in tongues that she didn't realize it's only one of the gifts of the Holy Spirit and that he had many more gifts for her and many fruits for her. She'd also become so convinced that everyone should speak in tongues that she'd spent her time trying to convince people they should have the gift. And consequently she was so busy majoring on a minor, as a friend put it, joy and love couldn't flow in her.

Now I don't condemn in any way the gift of tongues. My own experience indicates to me that it's an authentic gift, but my own experience also indicates that the Holy Spirit baptizes you in many ways. There are some who believe that if you don't speak in tongues, you haven't received the Holy Spirit. They try to get other persons to string some syllables together, thinking that this will start the flow of tongues. Or they try to work the person up emotionally so that in the emotion, he will start speaking in tongues. I know that some have been alienated by such insistence on using the gift of speaking in tongues as the only criterion for having received the Holy Spirit.

Rufus Moseley was one of the most delightful people I've ever met. The first time I heard him speak I was in college, and I thought he was the most joyful person I'd ever seen. When he spoke what he said was pure wisdom interspersed with such words and phrases as, "Glory"—"Praise you, Lord"—"Hallelujah"—"Thank you, Jesus"—"Have thine own way, Lord."

I wanted whatever it was that he had. And, according to him, what he had was union with Jesus. He got it through the baptism of the Holy Spirit. I was determined to have what he had, and I began to try to find out how to receive the Holy Spirit.

One night, several months later, I attended an E. Stanley Jones talk. Stanley Jones spoke on receiving the Holy Spirit. He made it sound so simple that I determined I wouldn't go to bed that night until I'd experienced the baptism.

When I returned to the dorm, my roommate was in tears. As we got ready for bed, she told me what was wrong. She said that she didn't like the job she had which helped pay her expenses at college and that she couldn't just quit it for she needed the money. We got into our beds and I said, "God has the perfect job just waiting for you and he'll lead you to it. Let's thank him that he's doing just that," and we took hands between our beds and began to thank God that he had the perfect job for her, when suddenly it was as though a great, glorious cloud which had been above and in front of me swooped down and flowed into me. I broke off the prayer and began to laugh with joy. I felt Jesus in my body, out to my fingertips and toes, and up to the top of my head. I said,

"Oh, I've got him! I've got him!" And I knew he'd live through me if I'd let him. It was a tremendous experience. Whereas when I'd walked to class or work or anywhere, I'd imagined Jesus walking beside me, talking with me, from then on, he was within.

Months went by and I heard that the receiving of the Holy Spirit is only the initial experience for the Christian, that there was more, much more, and I heard about speaking in tongues. I confess, I'm greedy. I wanted everything God would give me. I began to try to find out how I could receive the gift of tongues.

A small group of us from the college heard about a church where people spoke in tongues. We decided one night to go to it. There was a lovely service. During it, someone stood up and spoke in tongues, then sat down. Another person stood up and interpreted. At the end of the service, the pastor invited anyone who wanted to receive tongues to come to the front of the sanctuary and be prayed for. All of us went forward, and I knelt between two people who placed their hands on me and began to pray. The longer they prayed, the more uneasy I became. They started to shake my shoulders, and the sounds they made were harsh and guttural. It seemed as though they were trying to shake me into speaking in tongues. Yet nothing was happening in me except that I was getting more and more disgusted with the whole situation. All I wanted to do was get out of there as fast as I could. I thought, "If this is a gift, why does it seem to be so hard to receive it? Isn't it right here? Why are they shaking me? I want to get out of here." Then it entered my mind to praise God in French. I was minoring in French at the university, and it would be easy to pray a bit in French and maybe the people standing over me would let me get up and go. I said a few words in French, and the people above me rejoiced that I was speaking in tongues and they let me go. I headed outside to wait for the other young people. As I sat waiting for them I became angry that what I'd thought would be a great experience had turned out to be a flop. I thought that tongues was an emotionally induced experience and I wanted none of it.

Several days later I related my experience to an older friend of mine who led a prayer group. She said she'd experienced a similar thing, but that she'd finally gone to her bathroom, which was the only room in the house which had a lock. She locked the door, put the lid down on the commode, and sat on it. She'd said, "Lord, if there's anything to this speaking in tongues, I want to know it," and she waited. After a while she began quietly to speak in tongues. Then she knew there was something to it.

I thought, "If she can do it, so can I," and I went back to the dorm, locked the door of my room, pulled a chair out in front of the little prayer altar and picture of Jesus that my roommate and I had put up, and said, "OK, Lord, if there's anything to this, I want to know it." I waited, determined I wouldn't utter a sound. Anything that was to be said had to well up from within and flow out on its own. Slowly the room took on a feeling of warmth and I felt God's presence with me. Then I heard sounds coming out of my mouth. The syllables which came out were lovely. They sounded like an American Indian language. Finally I heard myself say, in English, "That's all." And as I sat quietly, the feeling of God's presence diminished. I knew, then, that there really was such an experience as speaking in tongues.

Since that time, I've often spoken in tongues, but I've been led not to do so with other people. The gift is for my own edification, as Paul says it is. I find that in deep moments of gratitude, when I'm praising God and just can't find enough words in the English language to tell him how much I love him, then it is that I go into tongues and feel a release inside which seems to say that I'm really telling God how I feel about him.

The gift of tongues has never been the most important thing in my life. Certainly it has made me feel closer to God, but I'd never insist that everybody should have this particular gift. I think it's best to open to God, to Jesus, the giver and keep your mind on him and then simply take whatever gifts come, remembering that it's more important to be one with the giver than to demonstrate the gifts.

Anything which takes our eyes off God, off Jesus,

can turn out to be a side road in our spiritual journey. It doesn't matter how good it is, tongues, prophecy, discernment, healing, or any other gift or fruit of the Spirit, if made central it pushes God to the periphery where he's unable to move in us and through us as he wants to do. But resolving to keep careful watch on ourselves and making sure that we place ourselves under the disciplines of prayer—above all practicing daily, hourly if need be, the rejoicing in God, in Jesus —and turning to him in thankfulness and praise, we can stay centered in him and can't be tempted to stay long on a side road.

As we live in the conscious presence of God, of Jesus, we begin to realize that love is working in and through us, love which draws us to the needs of the world. Perhaps the needs are in our own family or our church or our community, our nation, or the world. But we'll be led to them, and we'll discover God flowing through us in ways we didn't dream possible to meet those needs.

Right now, wherever you are, with whatever situation you are faced, begin to meet it with thanksgiving and gratitude. Offer it to Jesus, to God, and praise him that he's already begun to work it out. Each time you think of it, thank him again for taking care of it. Then ask him to help you see life from his perspective and thank him that he's beginning to do that for you. Praise and thank him for every little and big thing you can think of, and I can guarantee that there will come a time when your praise and thanksgiving won't be forced, but will begin to well up within you and flow from you in a well-nigh unbroken stream and then, union will come, union that will be a life-changing experience for you. There will come to you the re-sources of the vast universe to be channeled through you so that you know beyond a shadow of doubt that God and you are one and that in him you live cre-atively, joyously, and triumphantly. The ultimate glory of prayer can be yours—union with the Creator, Sustainer, Redeemer, Enabler.

Loving Father, Beloved Jesus, Blessed Holy Spirit, thank you for letting us share this time together through this book. You know the heart of this one who reads these words now. Open up the storehouse of heaven and let your blessings pour into him and let them find a warm reception. Help this person realize that you are as eager for union as he is and that at every step of his spiritual growth in prayer you'll be helping him. And bring him to that final, that ultimate, glory which is union with you. Amen.

SUGGESTIONS FOR ADDITIONAL READING

Bennett, Dennis J. *Nine O'clock in the Morning*. Plainfield, N. J.: Logos International, 1970.

Bro, Margueritte H. *More than We Are*. New York: Harper & Row, 1965.

Burkhart, Roy. *The Secret of Life*. New York: Harper & Brothers, 1950.

Clark, Glenn. *I Will Lift up Mine Eyes*. New York: Harper & Row, 1937.

——. *The Soul's Sincere Desire*. Boston: Little, Brown, 1925.

Cliffe, Albert. *Let Go and Let God*. New York: Prentice-Hall, 1951.

Day, Albert E. *An Autobiography of Prayer*. New York: Harper & Brothers, 1952.

——. *Discipline and Discovery*. Nashville: Upper Room, 1947.   :

Eggleston, Louise. Prayer Series and Subconscious Series. Norfolk, Va.: World Literacy Prayer Group, 1961.

Freer, Harold W. *Growing in the Life of Prayer*. Nashville: Abingdon Press ,1962.

Fromm, Erich. *The Art of Loving*. New York: Harper & Row, 1956.

Frost, Robert C. *Aglow with the Spirit*. Plainfield, N. J.: Logos International, 1965.

Jones, E. Stanley, *Growing Spiritually*. Nashville: Abingdon Press, 1954.

———. *In Christ*. Nashville: Abingdon Press, 1961.

Kelly, Thomas. *A Testament of Devotion*. New York: Harper & Row, 1941.

Laubach, Frank. *Channels of Spiritual Power*. New York: Harper & Brothers, 1942.

———. *Letters by a Modern Mystic*. Westwood, N.J.: Fleming H. Revell, 1937.

———. *You Are My Friends*. New York: Harper & Brothers, 1942.

Maltz, Maxwell. *Psycho-cybernetics: A New Way to Get More Living Out of Life*. New York: Prentice-Hall, 1960.

Murray, Andrew. *Abide in Christ*. New York: Grossett & Dunlap, 1968.

———. *With Christ in the School of Prayer*. Westwood, N. J.: Fleming H. Revell, 1965.

Ponder, Catherine. *The Dynamic Laws of Healing*. W. Nyack, N. Y.: Parker, 1966.

Sanford, Agnes. *Behold Your God*. St. Paul, Minn.: Macalester Park, 1958.

———. *The Healing Gifts of the Spirit*. Philadelphia: Lippincott, 1966.

———. *The Healing Light*. St. Paul, Minn.: Macalester Park, 1947.

———. *The Healing Power of the Bible*. Philadelphia: Lippincott, 1969.

Sherrill, John. *They Speak with Other Tongues*. New York: McGraw-Hill, 1964.

Smith, Hannah Whitehall. *The Christian's Secret of a Happy Life*. Westwood, N. J.: Fleming H. Revell, 1968.

Weatherhead, Leslie. *The Transforming Friendship*. Nashville: Abingdon Press, n.d.

———. *The Will of God*. Nashville: Abingdon Press, 1944.

Wyon, Olive. *The School of Prayer*. New York: The Macmillan Co., 1963.